Simply South

TRADITIONAL VEGETARIAN COOKING

Simply South

TRADITIONAL VEGETARIAN COOKING

CHANDRA PADMANABHAN

Food photography by N. Prabhaakkar

westland

westland ltd
Venkat Towers, 165, P.H. Road, Maduravoyal, Chennai 600 095
No. 38/10 (New No.5), Raghava Nagar, New Timber Yard Layout, Bangalore 560 026
Survey No. A - 9, II Floor, Moula Ali Industrial Area, Moula Ali, Hyderabad 500 040
23/181, Anand Nagar, Nehru Road, Santacruz East, Mumbai 400 055
4322/3, Ansari Road, Daryaganj, New Delhi 110 002

First published by westland ltd 2008

ISBN: 978-81-89975-74-6

Typeset in Gill Sans by Art Works, Chennai

Printed at Aditi Print-O-Fast, New Delhi

contents

This book is dedicated to
my darling grandson
Amithav Gautam

acknowledgements

1. Annapoorna Rama Rao Nuni
2. Aruna L Narayanan
3. Asha Hemdev
4. Chetna Mahabaleshwar
5. Chitra Iyengar
6. Jayalakshmi Narendranath
7. Jayanthi Ramesh
8. Leela Sekhar
9. Mallika Manickam
10. Mangalam Sridhar
11. Mythili Varadarajan
12. Nilanjana Roy
13. Sabita Radhakrishna
14. Saroja Sundaram
15. Sarojini Rajan
16. Sharada Rajamani
17. Sharanya Jaikumar
18. Sherna Wadia
19. Sreela Kowsik
20. Subashree Krishnaswamy
21. Sudha Hariharan
22. Sudha Prasad
23. Swati Prasad Siddharth
24. Usha Sundaram
25. Vijaya Subramanian

introduction

It is a popular belief that most people in South India are vegetarians. In fact this is not so; they constitute a very small minority and I happen to be one of them. All over the world more and more people are turning to vegetarianism for health reasons. When I started research for my two earlier books, I realized that South Indian vegetarian cooking was one of the most balanced cuisines in this part of the world.

Nutritionists the world over, believe that it is important to eat like a king at breakfast. It kick-starts your metabolism, and gives you the energy to cope with the day's work.

Traditionally, in South India, the previous day's leftover rice was soaked in water overnight; the water was drained, a little salt was added and the rice was mixed with curd or buttermilk, and eaten as breakfast. The dish is called pazhayadu. It is regarded as nutritious and this practice is still prevalent in some homes.

With the spread of education, an increasing number of people started migrating to cities to work. To make life easy, they started eating full-fledged meals by 9 a.m. in the morning, before catching a bus or train to work. The meal normally consisted of rice with sambar, rice with rasam, and rice with curd accompanied by a vegetable poriyal and a curd pachadi. Even today, some families eat such meals that resemble a lunch in the morning in place of breakfast.

As a result of Westernization and modernization, some of us have started eating a regular breakfast. Our breakfast tiffins are popular not only in the South, but all over India. The most popular tiffin is idli sambar with vadai, which is not only nutritious, but also light on the stomach. Today this tiffin is served on board aircrafts and trains, and it is available in most restaurants all over India. Other popular breakfast tiffins are dosai, masala dosai, oothappam, pongal, uppuma, appam and idiappam. There are innumerable ways of cooking these items, so one can never tire of them.

When I wrote my second book on South Indian cuisine, I came to the conclusion that I had more or less covered most of the popular South Indian recipes. However, since my earlier books were not published by Westland, my son Gautam, who heads this publishing house persuaded me to write a book for him. When I started researching for my third book, I came across some interesting dishes from Kongunadu, the North Arcot district of Tamil Nadu, Rajahmundry district of Andhra Pradesh and the Hebbar Iyengar community of Karnataka. This whetted my appetite for more information on these regions.

The name Arcot is derived from the Tamil words, aaru kaadu, meaning six forests, and the area is lush green. While studying the cuisine of this region, I discovered that they use wheat in their spice mixes. This intrigued me, since wheat is not indigenous to South India. Curiosity got the better of me, and further research revealed that the Mughal viceroys controlled this region at one point, and this probably explains the use of wheat. The famous pulliyogaray (tamarind rice), for example, is made with wheat lapsi and not rice, as in other parts of South India.

The Hebbar Iyengar community today, is a small one, and they are Vaishnavites. There are several theories regarding their origin. One theory claims they were local Kannadiga Brahmins who converted to Vaishnavism during Ramanujacharyar's stay at Melukote, while according to another theory, they migrated from Tamil Nadu, and others maintain that they were originally Jains. They speak a quaint language, which is a combination of Tamil and Kannada and their cuisine is unusual. I had provided their recipes for rice dishes like manga ogoray (mango rice) and ullundu ogoray (husked black gram rice), in my earlier books. Here I have included other dishes such as tengaipaal kuzhambu (coconut milk curry), kollukai satumadu (horse gram rasam), and ghasgase payasam (poppy seed dessert).

Rajahmundry lies in the Godavari delta in Andhra Pradesh. The area is rich in alluvial soil, and is called the rice bowl of Andhra Pradesh. With a vast variety of food growing in this region, it is well known for its delicious cuisine. High spices mark their dishes, and I have provided recipes for their famous pachadis (chutneys): allam pachadi (ginger chutney), aratikai pachadi (green plantain chutney) and menthukura pachadi (fenugreek leaf chutney). They make excellent dals: molapappu (curried mung), pesharattu kurma (dumpling curry); unusual rasams: mulakkada charu (drumstick rasam), cobbari paala pappucharu (coconut milk and lentil rasam): and a delicious payasam: paravaannam (rice dessert). Their snacks too differ from the usual south Indian fare: atukula dosai (parched rice pancake), challaatlu (sour curd pancake) and the famous pesharattu (mung pancake).

Kongunadu is the area around Coimbatore, Erode, Salem and Pollachi. It is located in the northwest of Tamil Nadu. The name is derived from the Kongu Vellala Gounder caste. The cuisine has a subtle flavour and is neither spicy nor oily. Copra is used in abundance, since plenty of coconut trees grow here, and turmeric is always added to their curries, giving them a rich colour.

Apart from these cuisines I have gathered other recipes from the four states of South India – Tamil Nadu, Andhra Pradesh, Karnataka and Kerala. Once again, I could only provide a sample from each state and community – a single book cannot do justice to all the districts and communities of South India.

I have had fun researching this book and hope you enjoy cooking from it.

Chandra Padmanabhan
Chennai (August 2008)

table of measures

metric	US / imperial
125 gms	4 oz
250 gms	8 oz
500 gms	16 oz (1 lb)
1 kg	32 oz (2 lb)

1 cup = 250 ml (8 fl oz) except in the US where it is 240 ml (7 fl oz)
1 tsp = 5 ml
1 tbsp = 3 tsp or 15 ml (½ fl oz) except in Australia where it is 20 ml
a pinch = ⅛ tsp (literally a pinch)
a dash = 1-2 drops
all spoon measures are level

Any small differences between metric, US and imperial measures have been absorbed, and will not affect the recipes.

Experienced cooks measure almost all ingredients by hand, while cooking Indian food. They know instinctively the right amounts required. To make it easy for the beginner I have measured most ingredients by volume – using the standard cups, tablespoons and teaspoons generally found in kitchens today – rather than by weight. I find this more convenient and time saving, as many of the ingredients used in the recipes are readily available in the kitchen.

In the case of vegetables that are usually stocked in the kitchen, like onions, potatoes, tomatoes, I have provided the number of vegetables required, while in cases where the vegetable may need to be especially bought for the dish being prepared, I have given the cup measure or weight.

As a rough guide, 100 gms of vegetables of the gourd family, plantains, yam, etc. would yield 1 cup when cut into ½" cubes.

A word of caution: while trying out a recipe, make sure you use the same measure for all the ingredients. For example, if a recipe requires three different types of flour, use the same cup to measure all three.

Throughout this book, the weight and measure equivalents given above have been used as standard.

south indian utensils you will require to make some of the dishes in this book

A few South Indian dishes in this book need special equipment to prepare them. These are readily available in South Indian stores around the country.

Idli rack: An idli rack or mould consists of a stand with plates fixed to it. Each plate has several depressions in them. Brush the depressions with oil and pour in about ¼ cup of idli batter into them. Place the rack in a pressure cooker and close the cooker. Steam idlies for 15-20 minutes, without putting the weight on. Let it cool for a few minutes and remove each idli from its depression with the help of a knife.

Appachatti: An appachatti is used to make appam. It is similar to a shallow wok, and has two handles and a lid. Heat the appachatti over moderate heat and smear evenly and lightly with oil, with the help of a piece of cloth. Pour a small ladle of appam batter into the centre of the pan. Quickly swirl the pan around, holding it with the handles to coat the sides and base of pan evenly with a thin layer of batter about 6" in diameter. Cover the pan and cook over low heat for 2-3 minutes. The base and edges of the appam should be golden, while the centre should be spongy. When the appam comes away from the sides, it is ready and you will be able to remove it from the chatti with a spatula.

Paniyaramchatti: Gundu pongla and moru appam can only be made in a paniyaram-chatti, which give these their typical rounded appearance. It is a frying pan that has several depressions in it. Place it over moderate heat and when hot, fill a quarter of each depression with oil. When the oil is hot, pour in batter to come halfway up the depression. Fry over low heat for 2-3 minutes. Gently turn the gundu pongla or moru appam with a skewer and fry the other side for 2-3 minutes till golden. Non-stick paniyaram chatti are available, in which case you need to use only ¼ tsp oil to coat the depressions, making the dishes healthier.

Thenkuzhal press (nazhi): This is a special press for making savoury crisps. It comes with changeable discs, which have holes of different sizes and shapes. The disc is placed at the base of a container and a piston with a handle fits snugly into it. Dough is filled into the container and the piston is fixed over it. The dough is pressed out through the holes in the disc by pushing down on the piston handle.

To make omappodi, choose a disc with several equally spaced tiny holes. For ribbon pakoda, change the disc to one which has two ½" slits running across its diameter. When dough is pressed through this disc, ribbon or tapeshaped crisps are formed.

Right : Clockwise from top left - idli stand, paniyaram chatti, appachatti and thenkuzhal press (nazhi), left disc - ribbon pakoda, right disc - omappodi

basic recipes

Left : Clockwise from top left - green cardamoms, black pappercorns, marathi moggu, cloves and cinnamon sticks

plain rice

I cup rice

Wash rice well and drain.

cooking in a pressure cooker
Place rice in a pressure cooker container with 2 cups water. Place container in cooker, along with sufficient water in the cooker. Close cooker and place over high heat. As steam starts escaping through the vent, cover vent with the weight. When the cooker reaches full pressure (the weight valve will whistle), lower heat and cook for 3 minutes.

Remove cooker from heat and allow pressure to fall on its own. This will take 15-20 minutes.

cooking on the stovetop
Place 2 cups water in a heavy-based pan over high heat and bring to boil. Add rice and bring to boil again. Lower heat to moderate and cook for 8-10 minutes, till water is almost absorbed.

Lower heat, place pan on a tawa or griddle, cover with a tight-fitting lid and cook for 7-8 minutes till water is absorbed and rice is tender and fluffy.

cooking in a microwave oven
Place rice with 2 cups water in a large casserole, twice as deep as the height of rice and water, so that the water does not boil over. Cover with a tight-fitting lid and cook on high for 6-7 minutes.

Cook on medium for 8-10 minutes or till all the liquid is completely absorbed. Allow to stand covered for 5 minutes.

chettinad rasam podi
rasam powder from chettinad

makes: about 1 cup
preparation time: 10 minutes
cooking time: 5 minutes

½ cup coriander seeds
1 tsp fenugreek seeds (methi)
¼ cup pigeon peas (tuvar/arhar)
2 tbsp oil
1 cup dried red chillies
1 tbsp cumin seeds
1 tbsp black peppercorns

1. Roast coriander seeds, fenugreek seeds and pigeon peas separately, in a dry frying pan over low heat, tossing gently, for a few moments. (Roast spices till fragrant and dal till it turns pink.) Set aside.

2. Heat oil in the same pan over low heat. Fry chillies, cumin seeds and peppercorns separately, tossing gently, till fragrant.

3. Cool and combine all ingredients. Grind to a fine powder.

4. Store in an airtight container and use as required.

rasam podi
rasam powder

makes: about 450 gms
preparation time: 15 minutes
cooking time: 5-7 minutes

1¼ cups (40 gms) dried red chillies
2½ cups (200 gms) coriander seeds
½ tbsp cumin seeds
½ cup (60 gms) black peppercorns
2 sprigs curry leaves
¾ cup (150 gms) pigeon peas (arhar/tuvar)
¼ cup (50 gms) husked bengal gram (chana dal)
1 tsp turmeric powder

1. Roast each ingredient, except turmeric powder, separately in a dry frying pan over low heat, tossing gently, for a few moments. (Roast chillies, spices and curry leaves till fragrant and dals till golden.)

2. Cool and combine all ingredients including turmeric powder. Grind to a fine powder.

3. Store in an airtight container and use as required.

sambar podi – 1
sambar powder

makes: about 2 cups
preparation time: 15 minutes
cooking time: 10 minutes

½ cup pigeon peas (tuvar/arhar)

½ cup husked bengal gram
(chana dal)

¼ cup husked black gram (urad dal)

½ cup cumin seeds

2 tbsp black peppercorns

2 tbsp fenugreek seeds (methi)

2½ cups coriander seeds

½ cup curry leaves

1 tbsp oil

2½ cups dried red chillies

2 tsp turmeric powder

1. Roast each ingredient separately, except oil, chillies and turmeric powder, in a dry frying pan over moderate heat, tossing gently, for a few moments. (Roast dals till golden and spices and curry leaves till fragrant.)

2. Add oil to the same pan and fry chillies, tossing gently, till fragrant

3. Cool and combine all ingredients including turmeric powder. Grind to a fine powder.

4. Store in an airtight container and use as required.

sambar podi – 2
sambar powder

makes: about 400 gms
preparation time: 20 minutes
cooking time: 5-7 minutes

2 cups (60 gms) dried red chillies

2 cups (140 gms) coriander seeds

¼ cup (30 gms) black peppercorns

¼ cup (25 gms) cumin seeds

2 tsp fenugreek seeds (methi)

2 tsp mustard seeds

2 tsp poppy seeds (khus-khus),
powdered

2 x 1" sticks cinnamon

½ cup (100 gms) curry leaves

½ cup husked bengal gram
(chana dal)

1 (40 gms) dry coconut (copra),
grated

2 tsp turmeric powder

1. Roast each ingredient, except turmeric powder, separately in a dry frying pan over low heat, tossing gently, for a few moments. (Roast chillies, spices and curry leaves till fragrant, and dal and copra till golden.)

2. Cool and combine all ingredients including turmeric powder. Grind to a fine powder.

3. Store in an airtight container and use as required.

sambar & kuzhambu

elumichampazham sambar
lemon curry

serves: 4-6
preparation time: 10 minutes
cooking time: 20 minutes

½ cup pigeon peas (arhar/tuvar)

2½ cups (500 gms) peeled and chopped (½" cubes) ridge gourd (toori)

2 medium-sized tomatoes, quartered

½ tsp turmeric powder

1 tsp salt or to taste

½ tsp asafoetida powder (hing)

3 tbsp lemon or lime juice

spice paste

1 tbsp coriander seeds

3-4 green chillies

2 tsp roasted bengal gram (bhuna chana)

2 tsp rice flour

1 cup grated fresh coconut

tempering

2 tsp ghee

½ tsp mustard seeds

½ tsp fenugreek seeds (methi)

1 tsp cumin seeds

1 dried red chilli, halved

1 sprig curry leaves

garnish

2 tbsp finely chopped coriander leaves

1. Wash dal and drain. Place dal in a pressure cooker with 1 cup water and cook under pressure for 5 minutes. Set aside.

2. Combine all ingredients for spice paste and grind to a smooth consistency gradually adding ½ cup water.

3. Boil 1 cup water in a wok/frying pan over high heat.

4. Mix in gourd, tomatoes, turmeric powder, salt and asafoetida powder. Lower heat, cover pan and simmer for 10 minutes till vegetables are tender.

5. Stir in spice paste and dal. Simmer uncovered for 5-7 minutes, stirring occasionally, till well blended.

6. Heat ghee for tempering in a small pan over moderate heat and add remaining ingredients for tempering in the order given. When mustard seeds splutter, stir contents of pan into sambar.

7. Add lemon or lime juice and mix well.

8. Garnish with coriander leaves.

9. Serve hot with plain rice.

chepankizhangu paruppu kuzhambu
colocasia and lentil curry

serves: 4-6
soaking time: 10 minutes
preparation time: 20 minutes
cooking time: 20 minutes

¾ cup pigeon peas (arhar/tuvar)
1½ cups (250 gms) colocasia
1 medium lemon-sized ball of tamarind
½ tsp turmeric powder
1 tsp salt or to taste
1 tsp rice flour (if required)

spice paste
2 tsp ghee
4-5 dried red chillies
3 tsp coriander seeds
½ tsp black peppercorns
1 tbsp grated dry coconut (copra)
1 tsp white sesame seeds (til)

tempering
2 tsp ghee
1 tsp mustard seeds
½ tsp fenugreek seeds (methi)
½ tsp cumin seeds
½ tsp asafoetida powder (hing)
1 dried red chilli, halved
1 sprig curry leaves

1. Wash dal and drain. Place dal in a pressure cooker with 1 cup water and cook under pressure for 5 minutes.

2. Boil colocasia in enough water to cover till tender. Drain, cool and peel. Slice colocasia into ½" pieces.

3. Soak tamarind in 1 cup water for 10 minutes. Extract juice and discard pulp.

4. Heat ghee for spice paste in a wok/frying pan and add remaining ingredients for spice paste. Fry over low heat, tossing gently, till fragrant. Grind to a smooth consistency, gradually adding 2-3 tbsp water.

5. To the same frying pan, add tamarind juice, turmeric powder and salt. Place pan over high heat and bring to boil. Lower heat and simmer for at least 10 minutes till the raw aroma of tamarind disappears.

6. Mix in dal, colocasia and spice paste. Simmer for about 5 minutes, stirring occasionally.

7. If kuzhambu is not thick enough, dissolve rice flour in ½ cup water and add to pan. Simmer for another 5 minutes, stirring frequently.

8. Heat ghee for tempering in a small pan over moderate heat. Add remaining ingredients for tempering in the order given. When mustard seeds splutter, stir contents of pan into kuzhambu.

9. Serve hot with plain rice.

keerai sambar
spinach curry

serves: 4-6
soaking time: 10 minutes
preparation time: 30 minutes
cooking time: 20 minutes

2 cups tightly packed spinach
leaves, finely chopped
½ tsp asafoetida powder (hing)
¼ tsp + 1 tsp salt
½ cup pigeon peas (arhar/tuvar)
¼ cup husked green gram
(mung dal)
1 tomato, quartered
½ tsp turmeric powder
1 medium lemon-sized ball of
tamarind
½" piece ginger, grated
6 green chillies, slit lengthwise
1 capsicum, cut into 1" squares
2 tsp sambar powder (page 14)

tempering
2 tsp oil
1 tsp mustard seeds
½ tsp fenugreek seeds (methi)
2 dried red chillies, halved
1 sprig curry leaves

garnish
1 tsp ghee
1 tsp coconut oil
2 tbsp finely chopped coriander
leaves

1. Combine spinach, asafoetida powder, ¼ tsp salt and 2-3 tbsp water in a pan and place over low heat. Cover pan and simmer for about 5 minutes till tender. Set aside.

2. Wash dals and drain. Place dals in a pressure cooker, with tomato, turmeric powder and 2 cups water. Cook under pressure for 5 minutes

3. Soak tamarind in 1 cup water for 10 minutes. Extract juice and discard pulp.

4. Heat oil for tempering in a wok/frying pan over moderate heat. Add remaining ingredients for tempering in the order given. When mustard seeds splutter, add ginger, green chillies and capsicum.

5. Stir in 1 tsp salt, tamarind juice and sambar powder. Lower heat and simmer for at least 10 minutes till the raw aroma of tamarind disappears.

6. Mix in spinach and simmer for about 2 minutes, stirring occasionally.

7. Add dal and simmer for about 5 minutes, stirring occasionally, till well blended.

8. Remove from heat and sprinkle ghee, coconut oil and coriander leaves on top.

9. Serve hot with plain rice.

vengaya sambar
shallot curry from palghat

serves: 4-6
soaking time: 10 minutes
preparation time: 30 minutes
cooking time: 30 minutes

2 drumsticks, cut into 3" pieces
1 medium lemon-sized ball of
tamarind
½ cup pigeon peas (tuvar/arhar)
1 cup (250 gms) shallots, peeled
and kept whole
1 tsp salt or to taste
½ tsp turmeric powder

spice paste
2 tsp + 2 tsp coconut oil
6 tbsp grated fresh coconut
2½ tbsp husked bengal gram
(chana dal)
6-8 dried red chillies
½ tsp fenugreek seeds (methi)
2 tbsp coriander seeds
½ tsp asafoetida powder (hing)

tempering
3 tbsp coconut oil
1 tsp mustard seeds
½ tsp fenugreek seeds (methi)
1 dried red chilli, halved
1 sprig curry leaves

garnish
2 tbsp finely chopped coriander
leaves

1. Bring 1 cup water to a boil over high heat. Add drumsticks and boil for 5-7 minutes, till tender. Set aside.

2. Soak tamarind in 1½ cups water for 10 minutes. Extract juice and discard pulp.

3. Wash dal and drain. Place dal in a pressure cooker, with 1 cup water. Cook under pressure for 5 minutes.

4. Heat 2 tsp oil for spice paste in a frying pan. Fry coconut over low heat, stirring continuously, till golden. Remove from pan and set aside.

5. Add 2 tsp oil to pan and add remaining ingredients for spice paste. Fry over low heat, tossing gently, till dal turns golden and chillies and spices are fragrant.

6. Combine all ingredients for spice paste and grind to a smooth consistency, gradually adding ½ cup water.

7. Heat oil for tempering in the same pan over moderate heat. Add remaining ingredients for tempering in the order given. When mustard seeds splutter, add shallots and fry till golden.

8. Stir in tamarind juice, salt and turmeric powder. Cover pan and simmer over low heat for at least 10 minutes, till the raw aroma of tamarind disappears.

9. Mix in spice paste and simmer for about 5 minutes, stirring occasionally.

10. Add drumsticks and dal, and simmer for at least 5 minutes, stirring occasionally, till well blended.

11. Garnish with coriander leaves.

12. Serve hot with plain rice. It can also be served as an accompaniment to idli, dosai and vadai.

avaraikkai araithuvitta sambar
sheet bean curry

serves: 4-6
soaking time: 10 minutes
preparation time: 20 minutes
cooking time: 20 minutes

¾ cup pigeon peas (tuvar/arhar)
1 medium lemon-sized ball of
tamarind
½ tsp turmeric powder
1 tbsp powdered jaggery
1½ tsp salt or to taste
1½ cups (200 gms) sliced
(½" pieces) sheet beans
1 medium-sized tomato, quartered

spice paste
3 tsp sesame oil (til ka tael)
1 tsp husked black gram
(urad dal)
1 tsp husked bengal gram
(chana dal)
4 dried red chillies
2 tsp coriander seeds
¾ tsp black peppercorns
½ tsp fenugreek seeds (methi)
½ tsp asafoetida powder (hing)
2 tbsp dry coconut (copra), grated
1 tsp rice grains

tempering
1 tbsp ghee
1 tsp mustard seeds
1 tsp cumin seeds
1 dried red chilli, halved
1 sprig curry leaves

garnish
2 tbsp finely chopped coriander
leaves

1. Wash dal and drain. Place dal in a pressure cooker with 1½ cups water. Cook under pressure for 5 minutes.

2. Soak tamarind in 1 cup water for 10 minutes. Extract juice and discard pulp.

3. Heat oil for spice paste in a frying pan. Add remaining ingredients for spice paste. Fry over low heat, tossing gently, till dals turn golden and chillies and spices are fragrant. Grind to a smooth consistency, gradually adding ½ cup water.

4. In the same pan, combine tamarind juice, turmeric powder, jaggery and salt. Place pan over high heat and bring to boil.

5. Add sheet beans and tomato. Lower heat, stir gently, cover pan and simmer for 10-12 minutes till the raw aroma of tamarind disappears and sheet beans are tender.

6. Mix in dal and spice paste. Add more water if sambar is too thick. Simmer for 5-7 minutes, stirring occasionally, till well blended.

7. Heat ghee for tempering in a small pan over moderate heat. Add remaining ingredients for tempering in the order given. When mustard seeds splutter, stir contents of pan into sambar.

8. Garnish with coriander leaves.

9. Serve hot with plain rice.

beetroot sambar
beetroot with lentils

serves: 4-6
soaking time: 10 minutes
preparation time: 10 minutes
cooking time: 25 minutes

¾ cup pigeon peas (tuvar/arhar)

1 medium lime-sized ball of tamarind

2 green chillies, slit

250 gms beetroot, peeled and cut into 1" cubes

½ tsp turmeric powder

2 tsp sambar powder (page 14)

1 tsp salt or to taste

tempering

2 tsp oil

1 tsp mustard seeds

½ tsp cumin seeds

½ tsp fenugreek seeds (methi)

½ tsp asafoetida powder (hing)

1 dried red chilli, halved

1 sprig curry leaves

garnish

2 tbsp finely chopped coriander leaves

1. Wash dal and drain. Place dal in a pressure cooker with 1½ cups water and cook under pressure for 5 minutes.

2. Soak tamarind in 1½ cups water for 10 minutes. Extract juice and discard pulp.

3. Combine tamarind juice, green chillies, beetroot, turmeric powder, sambar powder and salt in a pan. Place pan over high heat and bring to boil. Lower heat and simmer covered for 12-15 minutes, till the raw aroma of tamarind disappears and beetroot is tender.

4. Mix in dal and simmer uncovered for 5-7 minutes, stirring occasionally, till well blended.

5. Heat oil for tempering in a small pan over moderate heat. Add remaining ingredients for tempering in the order given. When mustard seeds splutter, stir contents of pan into sambar.

6. Garnish with coriander leaves and serve hot with plain rice.

verkadalay pitlay
peanut-flavoured curry

serves: 4-6
soaking time: 10 minutes
preparation time: 25 minutes
cooking time: 15 minutes

¼ cup pigeon peas (tuvar/arhar)

2 tbsp peanuts with skin

1 small lemon-sized ball of tamarind

4-5 (250 gms) aubergines (baingan), finely chopped

1 medium-sized tomato, finely chopped

1 tsp salt or to taste

½ tsp turmeric powder

spice paste

2 tsp oil

1 tsp husked black gram (urad dal)

5-6 dried red chillies

1 tbsp coriander seeds

½ tsp fenugreek seeds (methi)

1 tsp poppy seeds (khus-khus), powdered

½ tsp black peppercorns

2-3 tbsp grated fresh coconut

tempering

2 tsp oil

1 tsp mustard seeds

½ asafoetida powder (hing)

1 sprig curry leaves

1. Wash dal and drain. Place dal in a pressure cooker with ½ cup water and cook under pressure for 5 minutes.

2. Soak peanuts in ½ cup water for 10 minutes and drain.

3. Place peanuts with 2-3 tbsp water in a pan and cook covered over moderate heat for about 5 minutes, till tender. Drain and set aside.

4. Soak tamarind in ½ cup water for 10 minutes. Extract juice and discard pulp.

5. Heat oil for spice paste in a frying pan. Add remaining ingredients for spice paste. Fry over low heat, tossing gently, till dal turns golden and chillies and spices are fragrant.

6. Combine all ingredients for spice paste with peanuts. Grind to a fine consistency, gradually adding ½ cup water.

7. Heat 1 cup water in the same frying pan over moderate heat. Mix in aubergines, tomato, salt and turmeric powder. Lower heat and simmer for 8-10 minutes, stirring occasionally, till vegetables are tender.

8. Stir in tamarind juice and simmer for about 5 minutes.

9. Blend in dal and spice paste. Simmer for about 5 minutes, stirring occasionally.

10. Heat oil for tempering in a small pan over moderate heat. Add remaining ingredients for tempering in the order given. When mustard seeds splutter, stir contents of pan into pitlay.

11. Serve hot with plain rice.

karuvapillay kuzhambu
curry leaf tamarind curry

serves: 4-6
preparation time: 10 minutes
cooking time: 25-30 minutes

2 medium-sized tomatoes
¾ cup tightly packed curry leaves
1 small lemon-sized ball of
tamarind, without seeds or strings
1 tsp salt or to taste

tempering
2 tsp ghee
½ tsp mustard seeds
½ tsp asafoetida powder (hing)

spice paste
2 tsp ghee
½ tsp husked black gram
(urad dal)
1 tsp pigeon peas (tuvar/arhar)
5-6 dried red chillies
¾ tsp black peppercorns

1. Blanch tomatoes, peel and chop fine.

2. Heat ghee for tempering in a pan over moderate heat. Add remaining ingredients for tempering in the order given. When mustard seeds splutter, add tomatoes and fry for about 2 minutes. Remove from heat and set aside.

3. Heat ghee for spice paste in another pan. Add remaining ingredients for spice paste. Fry over low heat, tossing gently, till dals turn golden and chillies and spices are fragrant.

4. Combine fried spices with curry leaves, tamarind and salt. Grind to a smooth consistency, gradually adding ½ cup water.

5. Mix spice paste with 2 cups water in the same pan. Place pan over high heat and bring to boil. Blend in tempered tomatoes. Lower heat and simmer for about 25 minutes, stirring occasionally, till kuzhambu is thick, but has a pouring consistency.

6. Serve hot with plain rice.

vendakkai puli kuzhambu
tamarind-flavoured okra

serves: 4-6
soaking time: 10 minutes
preparation time: 15 minutes
cooking time: 20 minutes

*1 medium lemon-sized ball of
tamarind*
*1 cup (100-125 gms) sliced
(1" pieces) okra (bhindi)*
*1 medium-sized tomato, cut into
½" pieces*
½ tsp turmeric powder
2 tbsp powdered jaggery
1 tsp salt or to taste

spice paste
3 tsp sesame oil (til ka tael)
3-4 dried red chillies
½ tsp asafoetida powder (hing)
2 tsp coriander seeds
½ tsp fenugreek seeds (methi)
1 tsp white sesame seeds (til)
1 tsp husked black gram (urad dal)
1 tsp pigeon peas (tuvar/arhar)
*2 tsp husked bengal gram
(chana dal)*
2 tsp rice grains
2 tbsp grated fresh coconut

tempering
1 tbsp sesame oil
1 tsp mustard seeds
1 dried red chilli
1 sprig curry leaves

1. Soak tamarind in 2 cups water for 10 minutes. Extract juice and discard pulp.

2. Heat oil for spice paste in a frying pan. Add remaining ingredients for spice paste. Fry over low heat, tossing gently, till chillies and spices are fragrant and dals turn golden. Grind to a smooth consistency, gradually adding ¼ cup water.

3. Heat oil for tempering in the same frying pan over moderate heat. Add remaining ingredients for tempering in the order given. When mustard seeds splutter, add okra and sauté for about 2 minutes.

4. Blend in tomato and sauté for another minute.

5. Mix in tamarind juice, turmeric powder, jaggery and salt. Simmer covered over low heat for 12-15 minutes, stirring occasionally, till the raw aroma of tamarind disappears and vegetables are tender.

6. Mix spice paste with ½ cup water and pour into kuzhambu. Simmer for about 5 minutes, stirring occasionally, till well blended.

7. Serve hot with plain rice.

pakoda moru kuzhambu
dumpling curd curry

serves: 4-6
soaking time: 1 hour
preparation time: 20 minutes
cooking time: 25 minutes

pakoda

¾ cup husked bengal gram
(chana dal)

2-3 dried red chillies

¼ tsp asafoetida powder (hing)

½ tsp salt or to taste

oil for deep frying

spice paste

1 tsp pigeon peas (arhar/tuvar)

1 tsp husked bengal gram
(chana dal)

2 tsp oil

1¼ tsp husked black gram
(urad dal)

1 tsp fenugreek seeds (methi)

2-3 dried red chillies

2-3 green chillies

½" piece ginger, grated

3-4 tbsp grated fresh coconut

2 tbsp finely chopped coriander
leaves

moru kuzhambu

2 cups curd, whisked

1 tsp salt or to taste

½ tsp turmeric powder

tempering

2 tsp oil

1 tsp mustard seeds

½ tsp asafoetida powder (hing)

1 dried red chilli, halved

1 sprig curry leaves

pakoda

1. Wash dal and soak in 1½ cups water for 1 hour.
   Drain.

2. Combine dal with red chillies, asafoetida powder
   and salt. Grind to a thick, coarse batter, gradually
   adding 1 tbsp water.

3. Heat oil for deep frying in a frying pan over
   moderate heat. Drop spoonfuls of batter into oil
   and fry pakoda in batches, till golden. Drain and
   place on kitchen paper to absorb excess oil.

spice paste

4. Wash pigeon peas and bengal gram and soak in
   ½ cup water for 30 minutes.

5. Heat oil in a pan and add black gram, fenugreek
   seeds and red chillies. Fry over low heat, tossing
   gently, till dal turn golden.

6. Drain soaked dals and combine with fried spices
   and remaining ingredients for spice paste. Grind
   to a smooth consistency, gradually adding
   3-4 tbsp water.

moru kuzhambu

7. Whisk curd with salt and turmeric powder. Blend in
   spice paste.

8. Heat oil for tempering in a frying pan over
   moderate heat. Add remaining ingredients for
   tempering in the order given. When mustard seeds
   splutter, pour in curd mixture.

9. Cook over low heat for a few minutes, stirring
   continuously to prevent curdling.

10. Half an hour before serving, add pakoda to moru
    kuzhambu. Heat through and serve with rice.

tengaipaal moru kuzhambu
coconut milk and curd curry

serves: 4-6
soaking time: 10 minutes
preparation time: 20 minutes
cooking time: 30 minutes

1½ cups grated fresh coconut
2 cups fresh curd
½ tsp turmeric powder
1 tsp salt or to taste
2 medium-sized capsicums, cut
into ½" squares

spice paste
3 tsp ghee
1 green chilli
2-3 dried red chillies
3 tsp pigeon peas (tuvar/arhar)
¾ tsp black peppercorns
½ tsp asafoetida powder (hing)
2 tsp rice grains
1 tbsp grated fresh coconut

tempering
2 tsp sesame oil (til ka tael)
1 tsp mustard seeds
½ tsp fenugreek seeds (methi)
1 dried red chilli, halved
1 sprig curry leaves

1. Mix 1½ cups grated coconut with ¾ cup hot water. Process for 1-2 minutes in a blender. Pour liquid through a strainer lined with muslin cloth and press out coconut milk. Set aside.

2. Heat ghee for spice paste in a frying pan. Add all ingredients for paste, except coconut. Fry over low heat, tossing gently, till dal turns golden. Add coconut and toss for a few moments longer. Grind to a smooth consistency, gradually adding 2 tbsp water.

3. Place curd, turmeric powder, salt and spice paste in a bowl. Whisk till well blended and set aside.

4. Heat oil for tempering in a frying pan over moderate heat. Add remaining ingredients for tempering in the order given. When mustard seeds splutter, add capsicums and ¼ cup water. Cover pan and simmer over low heat for 5-7 minutes, stirring occasionally, till capsicums are tender.

5. Pour in curd mixture and heat through, stirring continuously.

6. Stir in coconut milk and remove from heat.

7. Mix well and serve hot with plain rice.

*Right : Molakeerai poritha kuzhambu
(Amarnath with lentils) see page 31*

vendaikai moru kuzhambu
okra and curd curry from north arcot

serves: 4-6
preparation time: 10 minutes
cooking time: 15 minutes

*250 gms okra (bhindi), cut into
1" slices*

2½ cups thick curd

½ tsp turmeric power

1 tsp salt or to taste

spice paste

*1 tbsp husked green gram
(mung dal)*

*1 tbsp husked bengal gram
(chana dal)*

1 tbsp pigeon peas (tuvar/arhar)

1 tsp husked black gram (urad dal)

1 tbsp wheat grains (gehun)

1 tbsp rice grains

3 dried red chillies

2 green chillies

1 tsp coriander seeds

½ tsp asafoetida powder (hing)

tempering

2 tsp oil

1 tsp mustard seed

1 sprig curry leaves

1. Roast all ingredients for spice paste on a dry frying pan over low heat. Toss gently, till dals turn golden and chillies and spices are fragrant. Grind to a smooth consistency, gradually adding ¼ cup water.

2. Heat oil for tempering in the same pan over moderate heat. Add mustard seeds and curry leaves. When mustard seeds splutter, add okra.

3. Sauté on low heat for 8-10 minutes till okra are tender. Sprinkle in 2 tbsp water while cooking.

4. Combine curd, turmeric powder, salt and spice paste in a bowl. Whisk well.

5. Add to okra and cook over low heat for a few minutes, stirring continuously to prevent curdling.

6. Serve hot with plain rice.

note: This is a delicious curd curry from the North Arcot district of Tamil Nadu. It is perfect for those who need to cut coconut from their diet.

*Left : Alu gaddé kuzhamb
(Potato curry from Karnataka) see page 39*

pushnikai moru kuzhambu
ash gourd and curd curry from thirunelveli

serves: 4-6
soaking time: 10 minutes
preparation time: 15 minutes
cooking time: 15 minutes

1 small marble-sized ball of
tamarind

1½ cups (250 gms) peeled and
chopped (1" cubes) ash gourd
(petha)

1 tsp salt or to taste

2 cups curd

spice paste

2 tsp oil

1 tsp husked black gram (urad dal)

¾ tsp fenugreek seeds (methi)

5-6 dried red chillies

¾ cup grated fresh coconut

tempering

2 tsp oil

1 tsp mustard seeds

1 sprig curry leaves

1. Soak tamarind in 1 cup water for 10 minutes. Extract juice and discard pulp.

2. Heat oil for spice paste in a frying pan. Add dal fenugreek seeds and red chillies and fry over low heat, tossing gently, till dal turns golden and chillies are fragrant. Mix in coconut and grind to a smooth consistency, gradually adding ½ cup water.

3. Add salt and spice paste to curd. Whisk till well blended and set aside.

4. Heat oil for tempering in a pan over moderate heat. Add mustard seeds and curry leaves. When mustard seeds splutter, mix in ash gourd and tamarind juice. Simmer over low heat for 5-7 minutes, stirring occasionally, till gourd is tender and the raw aroma of tamarind disappears.

5. Stir in spiced curd. Heat through, stirring continuously to prevent curdling.

6. Serve hot with plain rice.

mangai moru sambar
mango curd curry

serves: 4-6
preparation time: 20 minutes
cooking time: 10 minutes

¼ cup pigeon peas (tuvar/arhar)

1¼ cups grated fresh coconut

¾ cup finely chopped unripe mango

1 medium-sized tomato, finely chopped

1 tsp salt or to taste

½ cup fresh curd

spice paste

2 tsp oil

2 dried red chillies

1 tsp coriander seeds

½ tsp fenugreek seeds (methi)

4 small green chillies

1 tbsp roasted bengal gram (bhuna chana)

2 tbsp grated fresh coconut

tempering

2 tsp oil

1 tsp mustard seeds

½ tsp asafoetida powder (hing)

1 sprig curry leaves

1. Wash dal and drain. Place dal in a pressure cooker with ½ cup water and cook under pressure for 5 minutes.

2. Mix grated coconut with ½ cup hot water. Process for 1-2 minutes in a blender. Pour liquid through a strainer lined with muslin cloth and press out coconut milk.

3. Heat oil for spice paste in a frying pan. Add red chillies, coriander seeds and fenugreek seeds. Fry over low heat, tossing gently, till fragrant. Combine with remaining ingredients for spice paste and grind to a coarse consistency, gradually adding ¼ cup water.

4. Transfer cooked dal to a pan, add ½ cup water and whisk. Mix in mango, tomato and salt. Place pan over low heat and simmer for 8-10 minutes, stirring occasionally, till well blended. Remove from heat and add curd and coconut milk. Mix well.

5. Heat oil for tempering in a frying pan over moderate heat. Add remaining ingredients for tempering in the order given. When mustard seeds splutter, stir contents of pan into sambar.

6. Serve hot with plain rice.

note: The curd should not be even slightly sour for this dish.

tengai araitha kuzhambu
spicy coconut curry from tirunelveli

serves: 4-6
soaking time: 10 minutes
preparation time: 20 minutes
cooking time: 20 minutes

1 medium lime-sized ball of tamarind
1½ cups (500 gms) peeled and chopped (½" cubes) ash gourd (petha)
½ tsp turmeric powder
1 tsp salt or to taste

spice paste
1 tbsp oil
2 tbsp husked black gram (urad dal)
4 dried red chillies
¼ tsp fenugreek seeds (methi)
½ tsp white sesame seeds (til)
1¼ cups grated fresh coconut

tempering
1 tsp oil
½ tsp mustard seeds
1 sprig curry leaves

1. Soak tamarind in 2 cups water. Extract juice and discard pulp.

2. Combine tamarind juice, ash gourd, turmeric powder and salt in a pan placed over high heat and bring to boil. Lower heat and simmer for at least 10-12 minutes, stirring occasionally, till gourd is tender and the raw aroma of tamarind disappears.

3. Heat oil for spice paste in a frying pan. Add remaining ingredients for paste, except coconut. Fry over low heat, tossing gently, till dal turns golden and chillies and spices are fragrant. Mix in coconut and grind to a smooth consistency, gradually adding ½ cup water.

4. Add spice paste to cooked ash gourd. Mix gently and simmer over low heat for 4-5 minutes, stirring occasionally, till well blended.

5. Heat oil for tempering in a small pan over moderate heat. Add mustard seeds and curry leaves. When mustard seeds splutter pour contents of pan into kuzhambu.

6. Serve hot with plain rice.

molakeerai poritha kuzhambu
amaranth with lentils

serves: 4-6
preparation time: 20 minutes
cooking time: 15 minutes

½ cup pigeon peas (tuvar/arhar)

4-5 cups amaranth leaves, cleaned and finely chopped

1 medium-sized tomato, quartered

1 tsp salt or to taste

spice paste

2 tsp oil

2 tsp husked black gram (urad dal)

2 dried red chillies

½ tsp black peppercorns

½ tsp cumin seeds

2 tsp coriander seeds

½ tsp asafoetida powder (hing)

4-5 tbsp grated fresh coconut

tempering

2 tsp ghee

1 tsp mustard seeds

1 tsp husked black gram

1 dried red chilli, halved

1 sprig curry leaves

1. Wash dal and drain. Place dal in a pressure cooker with 1 cup water. Cook under pressure for 5 minutes.

2. Heat oil for spice paste in a frying pan. Add remaining ingredients for spice paste, except coconut. Fry over low heat, tossing gently, till dal turns golden and chillies and spices are fragrant. Mix in coconut and grind to a smooth consistency, gradually adding ¼ cup water.

3. Place amaranth and tomato in a frying pan with ¼ cup water. Cover pan, place over low heat and simmer for 3-5 minutes, till vegetables are tender.

4. Blend in cooked dal, salt and spice paste. Add more water if kuzhambu is too thick. Simmer uncovered over low heat, stirring occasionally, for 5-7 minutes, till well blended.

5. Heat ghee for tempering in a small pan over moderate heat. Add remaining ingredients for tempering in the order given. When mustard seeds splutter, stir contents of pan into kuzhambu.

6. Serve hot with plain rice.

peerkangai beans kootu kuzhambu
ridge gourd with french beans

serves: 4-6
soaking time: 10 minutes
preparation time: 20 minutes
cooking time: 25 minutes

⅓ cup pigeon peas (tuvar/arhar)

1 medium lemon-sized ball of tamarind

½ tsp turmeric powder

1 tsp salt or to taste

2 cups peeled, chopped (½" cubes) ridge gourd (toori)

1 cup sliced (½" pieces) french beans

1 medium-sized tomato, quartered

1 tbsp powdered jaggery

spice paste

3 tsp oil

1 tsp husked black gram (urad dal)

2 tsp husked bengal gram (chana dal)

4 dried red chillies

3 tsp coriander seeds

½ tsp black peppercorns

½ tsp asafoetida powder (hing)

2 tsp rice grains

4 tbsp grated fresh coconut

tempering

2 tsp ghee

1 tsp mustard seeds

½ tsp cumin seeds

1 dried red chilli, halved

1 sprig curry leaves

1. Wash dal and drain. Place dal in a pressure cooker with ¾ cup water. Cook under pressure for 5 minutes.

2. Soak tamarind in 1 cup water for 10 minutes. Extract juice and discard pulp.

3. Heat oil for spice paste in a frying pan. Add remaining ingredients for spice paste. Fry over low heat, tossing gently, till dals turns golden and chillies and spices are fragrant. Grind to a smooth consistency, gradually adding ¼ cup water.

4. Place turmeric powder, salt, ridge gourd, French beans and tomato with 2 cups water in the same pan and bring to boil over high heat. Lower heat and simmer uncovered for 8-10 minutes, stirring occasionally, till vegetables are tender.

5. Mix in tamarind juice and jaggery. Simmer uncovered for 5-7 minutes.

6. Stir in cooked dal and spice paste. Simmer for another 5-7 minutes, stirring occasionally, till well blended.

7. Heat oil for tempering in a small pan over moderate heat and add remaining ingredients for tempering in the order given. When mustard seeds splutter, stir contents of pan into kuzhambu.

8. Serve hot with plain rice.

nurge gashie
spicy drumsticks from mangalore

serves: 4-6
preparation time: 10 minutes
cooking time: 25 minutes

1 tsp salt or to taste
7-8 drumsticks, cut into 2" pieces
1 tbsp powdered jaggery
1 medium-sized onion, finely chopped

spice paste
2 tsp oil
5-6 dried red chillies
3 tbsp coriander seeds
½ tsp fenugreek seeds (methi)
1 tsp husked black gram (urad dal)
¾ tsp black peppercorns
1 tsp cumin seeds
1 medium lemon-sized ball of tamarind, without seeds or strings
2-3 cloves garlic (optional)
½ tsp turmeric powder
1 cup grated fresh coconut

tempering
2 tbsp oil
1 tsp mustard seeds
1 tsp cumin seeds
1 tsp husked black gram
1 sprig curry leaves

garnish
2 tbsp finely chopped coriander leaves

1. Place 2 cups water with salt in a frying pan over high heat and bring to boil. Add drumsticks, lower heat and simmer for 10 minutes till tender. Set aside with its cooking liquid.

2. Heat oil for spice paste in a pan. Add red chillies, coriander seeds, fenugreek seeds and dal. Fry over low heat, tossing gently till chillies and spices are fragrant and dal turns golden.

3. Combine fried ingredients with remaining ingredients for spice paste. Grind to a smooth consistency, gradually adding ½ cup water.

4. Add jaggery and spice paste to pan containing drumsticks. Mix gently and place pan over low heat. Simmer for about 10 minutes, stirring occasionally, till well blended.

5. Heat oil for tempering in a small pan over moderate heat. Add remaining ingredients for tempering in the order given. When mustard seeds splutter, add onion and fry till golden. Pour contents of pan over gashie.

6. Garnish with coriander leaves and serve hot with plain rice or roti.

karamani kuzhambu
cowpeas with aubergine from kongunadu

serves: 4-6
soaking time: 10 minutes
preparation time: 20 minutes
cooking time: 20 minutes

½ cup cowpeas (lobia)

1 marble-sized ball of tamarind

3-4 aubergines (baingan), sliced lengthwise

1 tsp salt or to taste

½ tsp turmeric powder

2 green chillies, slit lengthwise

ground to a paste

1 tsp cumin seeds

2 dried red chillies

4 tbsp grated fresh coconut

1-2 tbsp water

tempering

1 tsp oil

½ tsp mustard seeds

1 tsp husked black gram (urad dal)

1 sprig curry leaves

1. Wash cowpeas and drain. Place cowpeas in a pressure cooker with 1 cup water. Cook under pressure for 7 minutes.

2. Soak tamarind in 1½ cups water for 10 minutes. Extract juice and discard pulp.

3. Combine tamarind juice, aubergines, salt and turmeric powder in a pan over high heat and bring to boil. Lower heat and simmer for 8-10 minutes, stirring occasionally, till the raw aroma of tamarind disappears and aubergines are tender.

4. Mix in cooked cowpeas, green chillies and spice paste. Simmer over low heat for 5-7 minutes, stirring occasionally, till well blended.

5. Heat oil for tempering in a small pan over moderate heat. Add remaining ingredients for tempering in the order given. When mustard seeds splutter, pour contents of pan into kuzhambu. Mix well.

6. Serve hot with plain rice.

pagarkai pitlay
bitter gourd curry from kongunadu

serves: 4-6
soaking time: 8 hours
preparation time: 20 minutes
cooking time: 20 minutes

½ cup whole bengal gram (kala chana)

1 small lemon-sized ball of tamarind

1 cup sliced (¼" rounds) bitter gourd (karela)

½ tsp turmeric powder

1 tsp salt or to taste

ground to a paste
3 tbsp grated fresh coconut

¾ tsp cumin seeds

4-5 shallots, peeled

3 dried red chillies

¼ cup water

tempering
1 tsp oil

½ tsp mustard seeds

1 tsp husked black gram (urad dal)

1 sprig curry leaves

1. Wash gram and soak in 1 cup water for 8 hours. Drain gram and rinse well. Place gram in a pressure cooker with 1 cup water. Cook under pressure for 5 minutes.

2. Soak tamarind in 1½ cups water for 10 minutes. Extract juice and discard pulp.

3. Place tamarind juice, bitter gourd, turmeric powder and salt in a pan over moderate heat and bring to boil. Lower heat and simmer for 8-10 minutes, stirring occasionally, till the raw aroma of tamarind disappears and gourd is tender.

4. Mix in cooked gram and ground paste. Simmer for another 5 minutes, stirring occasionally, till well blended.

5. Heat oil for tempering in a small pan over moderate heat. Add remaining ingredients for tempering in the order given. When mustard seeds splutter, pour contents of pan into pitlay.

6. Serve hot with plain rice.

tengai paal kuzhambu
coconut milk curry from the hebbar iyengar community of karnataka

serves: 4-6
preparation time: 20 minutes
cooking time: 15 minutes

2 cups grated fresh coconut
2½ cups (500 gms) peeled and chopped (½" cubes) ridge gourd (toori)
1 tsp salt or to taste

spice paste
1 tsp husked black gram (urad dal)
¼ tsp black peppercorns
2 tbsp grated fresh coconut

1. Roast dal and black peppercorns for spice paste in a dry frying pan over low heat, tossing gently, till dal turns pink. Mix in coconut and grind to a smooth consistency, gradually adding 1 tbsp water.

2. Mix grated coconut with 1 cup hot water. Process for 1-2 minutes in a blender. Pour liquid through a strainer lined with muslin cloth and press out thick coconut milk.

3. Add 1 cup hot water to coconut residue. Blend and strain once more to extract thin coconut milk.

4. Combine ridge gourd and thin coconut milk in a pan over moderate heat and bring to boil. Lower heat and simmer for 8-10 minutes till tender.

5. Add spice paste and simmer, stirring to blend, for about 2 minutes.

6. Mix in thick coconut milk and heat through for 1-2 minutes, stirring continuously.

7. Serve hot with rice.

molapappu
curried mung from andhra pradesh

serves: 4-6
soaking time: 30 minutes
preparation time: 10 minutes
cooking time: 35 minutes

1 cup husked green gram
(mung dal)
2 large onions, finely chopped
2 green chillies, slit lengthwise
2 tsp red chilli powder
½ tsp turmeric powder
1 tsp salt or to taste

tempering
2 tbsp oil
1 sprig curry leaves

ground to a smooth paste
2 green cardamoms
3-4 cloves
1" stick cinnamon
2 tsp coriander seeds
3 tsp poppy seeds (khus-khus),
powdered
1½" piece ginger, grated
½ tsp cumin seeds
3-4 cloves garlic (optional)
¼ cup water

garnish
2 tbsp finely chopped coriander
leaves

1. Wash dal and soak in 2 cups water for 30 minutes.

2. Heat oil for tempering in a frying pan over moderate heat. Add curry leaves, onions and green chillies and fry till onions are golden. Sprinkle in chilli powder, turmeric powder and salt. Fry for another 30 seconds.

3. Add 4 cups water and bring to boil. Drain dal and add to pan. Lower heat and simmer for 25 minutes till dal is tender, taking care it does not turn mushy.

4. Mix spice paste with ½ cup water and stir into dal. Simmer for 4-5 minutes, stirring occasionally, till well blended.

5. Garnish with coriander leaves and serve hot with roti or rice.

theeyal
aubergine curry from kerala

serves: 4-6
soaking time: 10 minutes
preparation time: 15 minutes
cooking time: 20 minutes

1 medium lime-sized ball of
tamarind
1 tsp coconut oil
½ tsp turmeric powder
1½ cups (250 gms) sliced (1" slices,
lengthwise) small aubergines
(baingan)
6 green chillies, slit lengthwise
2-3 shallots, peeled and kept
whole
1½ tsp salt or to taste

spice paste
4 dried red chillies
1 tsp coriander seeds
2-3 shallots, peeled
2 cups grated fresh coconut

tempering
1½ tbsp coconut oil
½ tsp mustard seeds
2 dried red chillies, halved
2-3 shallots, sliced
1 sprig curry leaves

1. Soak tamarind in 2 cups water for 10 minutes. Extract juice and discard pulp.

2. Roast ingredients for spice paste separately in a dry frying pan, tossing gently, over low heat. (Roast chillies and coriander seeds till fragrant, and shallots and coconut till golden.)

3. Cool and combine all ingredients for spice paste. Grind to a smooth consistency, gradually adding 1¼ cups water.

4. Heat 1 tsp oil in the same pan. Sprinkle in turmeric powder and sauté for 20 seconds over low heat.

5. Add aubergines, green chillies and shallots and give it a stir. Mix in tamarind juice and salt. Simmer over low heat for at least 10-12 minutes, stirring occasionally till the raw aroma of tamarind disappears.

6. Blend in spice paste and simmer for 5-7 minutes, stirring occasionally till gravy thickens.

7. Heat oil for tempering in a small pan over moderate heat. Add remaining ingredients for tempering in the order given. When mustard seeds splutter and shallots turn golden, pour contents of pan into theeyal.

8. Serve hot with plain rice.

alu gaddé kozhamb
potato curry from karnataka

serves: 4-6
preparation time: 15 minutes
cooking time: 10 minutes

5-6 (500 gms) medium-sized
potatoes
⅓ cup pigeon peas (arhar/tuvar)
1 tsp salt or to taste
1 green chilli, slit lengthwise
½ cup milk
1 sprig curry leaves

ground to a paste
¾ cup grated fresh coconut
1 tsp mustard seeds
3-4 dried red chillies
1 tbsp rice grains
¼ tsp turmeric powder
½ cup water

1. Boil potatoes, peel and cut into ½" cubes.

2. Wash dal and drain. Place dal in a pressure cooker with ¾ cup water. Cook under pressure for 5 minutes.

3. Combine potatoes, dal, salt, green chilli and spice paste in a pan placed over low heat. Add milk and simmer for 5-8 minutes, stirring occasionally till well blended.

4. Add curry leaves just before removing from heat.

5. Serve hot with plain rice.

variation: Use 1 cup shelled green peas or a bunch of finely chopped spinach instead of potatoes.

masala vadai kulambu
curried patties from the mudaliar community

serves: 4-6
soaking time: 2 hours
preparation time: 30 minutes
cooking time: 50 minutes

masala vadai

*1 cup husked bengal gram
(chana dal)*

*2 medium-sized onions, finely
chopped*

4 green chillies, finely chopped

1" piece ginger, grated

½ tsp salt or to taste

2 cups oil

kulambu

1 small lime-sized ball of tamarind

½ tsp turmeric powder

2 tsp coriander powder

2 tsp red chilli powder

*1 medium-sized onion, finely
chopped*

6 cloves garlic, finely chopped

2 sprigs curry leaves

*1 medium-sized tomato, finely
chopped*

1 tsp salt or to taste

tempering

3 tbsp sesame oil (til ka tael)

*1 tbsp vadagam (see note
on page 41)*

or

*½ tsp mustard seeds
+ ½ tsp husked black gram
(urad dal)*

masala vadai

1. Wash dal, soak in water for 2 hours and drain. Grind dal coarsely, gradually adding 3-4 tbsp water. Add onions, green chillies, ginger and salt. Mix well.

2. Heat oil in a deep frying pan to smoking point.

3. Wet your hands, take a ladle of batter and flatten it into a 1" round patty. Slip it gently into hot oil. Fry vadai in batches over moderate heat, turning frequently, till golden brown and crisp. Drain and place on kitchen paper to absorb excess oil.

kulambu

4. Soak tamarind in 2 cups water for 10 minutes. Extract juice and discard pulp.

5. Add 2½ cups water to tamarind juice, with turmeric powder, coriander powder and chilli powder. Mix well and set aside.

6. Heat oil for tempering in a pan over moderate heat. Add vadagam or other ingredients for tempering and fry for 30 seconds. When vadagam or mustard seeds splutter, add onion, garlic and curry leaves.

7. Fry for 3-4 minutes, stirring continuously.

8. Blend in tomato and fry for a 1-2 minutes.

9. Add spiced tamarind juice and salt. Mix well and simmer over low heat for at least 15-18 minutes, stirring occasionally, till the raw aroma of tamarind disappears.

10. Gently mix in coconut paste and simmer over low heat for 3-5 minutes, stirring occasionally, till well blended.

11. Add vadai, one at a time, and simmer for 2-3 minutes. Remove from heat.

12. Serve hot with rice.

+ ½ tsp fenugreek seeds (methi)
+ ½ tsp fennel seeds (saunf)

ground to a smooth paste
½ cup grated fresh coconut
2 tsp poppy seeds (khus-khus),
powdered
2-3 tbsp water

note: Vadagam is a tempering ingredient ground and compressed into sun-dried lime-sized balls. It is commercially available in grocery stores selling South Indian food items. It is commonly used by the Mudaliar community of Tamil Nadu.

pesharattu kurma
dumpling curry from andhra pradesh
You will need an idli rack (described on page 10) to prepare this dish.

serves: 4-6
soaking time: 1½ hours
preparation time: 10 minutes
cooking time: 40 minutes

bean dumplings
1 cup whole mung (sabut mung)
2 green chillies
¾ tsp salt or to taste
3 tbsp oil

kurma
3 tbsp oil
1 green cardamom
2 cloves
½" stick cinnamon
1 tsp red chilli powder
½ tsp turmeric powder
¾ tsp salt or to taste
2 tbsp milk

ground to a coarse paste
½ tsp cumin seeds
4 cloves garlic (optional)
2 onions, chopped roughly

garnish
2 tbsp chopped coriander leaves

1. Wash mung and soak in water for 1½ hours. Rinse well and drain thoroughly.

2. Grind green chillies to a paste. Mix chilli paste with soaked mung and salt. Grind to a coarse batter, gradually adding ½ cup water.

3. Brush an idli rack with oil. Spoon ¼ cup batter into each depression. Place rack in a pressure cooker. Close cooker and steam for 15-20 minutes (without weight). Loosen idli from rack. Cool and cut into 1" pieces.

4. Heat 3 tbsp oil in a frying pan. Fry dumplings in batches, lightly over moderate heat for 4-5 minutes. Drain and set aside.

5. Add oil for kurma to the same pan and place on moderate heat. Toss in cardamom, cloves and cinnamon and give it a stir. Add spice paste and fry till golden brown.

6. Sprinkle in chilli powder, turmeric powder, salt and 1½ cups water. Mix well, lower heat and simmer for 8-10 minutes, stirring occasionally, till well blended.

7. Add dumplings and simmer for 4-5 minutes. When moisture is almost absorbed, mix in milk and simmer over low heat for 1-2 minutes. The curry should be moist, and not completely dry.

8. Garnish with chopped coriander leaves.

9. Serve hot with plain rice or roti.

note: Batter left over after making pesharattu (page 116), can also be used to make the dumplings for this curry.

variation: Instead of making idli with the batter, make a thick dosai, cut into 1" pieces and add to the kurma.

Right : Cobri paalapappu charu
(Coconut milk and lentil rasam from Andhra Pradesh) see page 56

nalagree
vegetable curry

This is a delicious kuzhambu made by the hebbar iyengar community of karnataka.

serves: 4-6
soaking time: 8 hours
preparation time: 30 minutes
cooking time: 20 minutes

¾ *cup cowpeas (lobia)*

¾ *cups pigeon peas (tuvar/arhar)*

1 medium lime-sized ball of tamarind

2 cups (500 gms) peeled and chopped (1" cubes) ash gourd (petha)

1 tsp salt or to taste

spice paste

2 dried red chillies

1 tbsp coriander seeds

½ tsp fenugreek seeds (methi)

¼" stick cinnamon

*1 marathi moggu
(optional – see note alongside)*

*½ tbsp husked bengal gram
(chana dal)*

*½ tsp husked black gram
(urad dal)*

2 tbsp grated fresh coconut

tempering

2 tsp oil

1 tsp mustard seeds

½ tsp asafoetida powder (hing)

1 medium-sized onion, finely chopped

1. Wash cowpeas and soak in 1½ cups water for 8 hours. Drain cowpeas, rinse thoroughly and place in a pressure cooker with 1 cup water. Cook under pressure for 5 minutes.

2. Wash pigeon peas and drain. Place pigeon peas in a pressure cooker with 1½ cups water. Cook under pressure for 3 minutes.

3. Soak tamarind in 1 cup water for 10 minutes. Extract juice and discard pulp.

4. Place 1 cup water in a pan over high heat and bring to boil. Add ash gourd, cover pan and simmer over low heat for 5-7 minutes till tender. Set aside with its cooking liquid.

5. Roast all ingredients for spice paste, except coconut, separately in a dry frying pan over low heat, tossing gently. (Roast chillies and spices till fragrant and dals till golden.)

6. Combine roasted ingredients with coconut and grind to a smooth consistency, gradually adding ¼ cup water.

7. Transfer cowpeas and dal to a frying pan. Mix in tamarind juice, ash gourd with its cooking liquid and salt. Simmer over low heat for 5-7 minutes, stirring occasionally, till well blended.

8. Blend in spice paste and simmer, stirring occasionally, for 3-4 minutes.

9. Heat oil for tempering in a small pan over moderate heat and add mustard seeds and asafoetida powder. When mustard seeds splutter, add onion and fry till golden. Stir contents of pan into nalagree.

10. Serve hot with plain rice.

note: Marathi moggu is a spice resembling a large clove that is commonly used in Karnataka cuisine.

variation: Instead of ash gourd use chopped potatoes, aubergines or french beans. They taste equally delicious.

*Left : Kosu carrot rasam
(Cabbage and carrot rasam) see page 54*

mirchi ka salan
green chilli curry from hyderabad

serves: 4-6
soaking time: 10 minutes
preparation time: 10 minutes
cooking time: 20 minutes

This is a popular curry from hyderabad, made with a special variety of chillies which are used to make fritters or bhajia.

250 gms (12) large, mild green chillies

1 tsp salt + ½ tsp or to taste

1 medium lemon-sized ball of tamarind

¼ cup oil

1 tsp cumin seeds

½ tsp asafoetida powder (hing)

1 sprig curry leaves

1 tbsp finely chopped mint leaves

½ tsp turmeric powder

spice paste
3 large onions

2-3 cloves garlic (optional)

1 large tomato

1" piece ginger

spice powder
1 tbsp oil

½ tsp nigella seeds (kalaunji)

1 tbsp grated dry coconut (copra)

1 tbsp poppy seeds (khus-khus)

1 tbsp black sesame seeds (til)

1 tbsp raw peanuts

garnish
2 tbsp finely chopped coriander leaves

1. Slit chillies lengthwise keeping stalks intact. Remove seeds carefully without separating the segments.

2. Bring 1 cup water to boil with 1 tsp salt in a pan over high heat. Add chillies and blanch for a minute. Drain well and set aside. Reserve water.

3. Soak tamarind in 2 cups water for 10 minutes. Extract juice and discard pulp.

4. Mix all ingredients for spice paste and grind to a smooth consistency, gradually adding 2-3 tbsp reserved chilli water.

5. Heat oil for spice powder in a pan. Add remaining ingredients for spice powder. Fry over low heat, tossing gently, till spices are fragrant and copra is golden. Cool and grind to a fine powder.

6. Heat ¼ cup oil in the same pan over moderate heat. Fry blanched chillies for 2-3 minutes. Remove from pan, drain and set aside.

7. Add cumin seeds, asafoetida powder, curry leaves and mint leaves to pan. When cumin seeds splutter, sprinkle in turmeric powder and fry for a minute, stirring continuously.

8. Blend in spice paste and fry for 2-3 minutes, stirring continuously. Mix in spice powder and stir-fry for another 2-3 minutes.

9. Add fried chillies, tamarind juice and ½ tsp salt. Stir gently to blend ingredients and simmer over low heat for 12-15 minutes, stirring occasionally, till oil floats to the surface and curry is aromatic.

10. Garnish with chopped coriander leaves and serve with zaffrani vegetable pulao (page 98) or roti.

rasam

mulakkada charu
drumstick rasam from andhra pradesh

serves: 4-6
soaking time: 10 minutes
preparation time: 5 minutes
cooking time: 20 minutes

*1 medium lemon-sized ball of
tamarind*

1 drumstick, cut into 3" pieces

½ tsp turmeric powder

1 tsp red chilli powder

1 tsp salt or to taste

*½ medium-sized onion or
2 shallots, finely chopped*

1 tbsp grated jaggery

tempering

2 tsp oil

½ tsp mustard seeds

½ tsp cumin seeds

¼ tsp fenugreek seeds (methi)

½ tsp asafoetida powder (hing)

1 sprig curry leaves

1. Soak tamarind in 1 cup water for 10 minutes. Extract juice and discard pulp.

2. Add 3 cups water to tamarind juice and pour into a pan. Add drumstick, turmeric powder, chilli powder, salt, onion or shallots and jaggery. Mix well, place pan over high heat and bring to boil. Lower heat and simmer for 12-15 minutes, till rasam is reduced to 2 cups, stirring occasionally.

3. Heat oil for tempering in a pan over moderate heat. Add remaining ingredients for tempering in the order mentioned. When mustard seeds splutter stir contents of pan into rasam.

4. Serve hot with rice.

note: This rasam is normally served with dal (tuvar/arhar) and rice.

variation: Use okra (bhindi) instead of drumsticks.

kollukai satumadu
horse gram rasam from the
hebbar iyengar community of karnataka

serves: 4-6
soaking time: 8-9 hours
preparation time: 30 minutes
cooking time: 20 minutes

2 tbsp horse gram (kulthi ka dal)
2 tbsp pigeon peas (tuvar/arhar)
1 marble-sized ball of tamarind
2 tsp rasam powder (page 13)
½ tsp asafoetida powder (hing)
1 tsp salt or to taste

tempering
2 tsp ghee
½ tsp mustard seeds
1 tsp cumin seeds
1 dried red chilli, halved
1 sprig curry leaves

1. Wash horse gram and soak in 1 cup water for 8-9 hours. Drain and rinse thoroughly. Wash pigeon peas and drain. Place both dals in a pressure cooker with 1½ cups water and cook under pressure for 5 minutes.

2. Soak tamarind in 1 cup water for 10 minutes. Extract juice and discard pulp.

3. Place tamarind juice, rasam powder, asafoetida powder and salt in a pan over moderate heat. Bring to boil. Lower heat and simmer for at least 10 minutes, till the raw aroma of tamarind disappears.

4. Add cooked dals and simmer, stirring occasionally, for another 5-7 minutes. Pour in 1 cup water if rasam is too thick.

5. Heat ghee for tempering in a pan over moderate heat. Add remaining ingredients for tempering in the order given. When mustard seeds splutter, pour contents of pan into rasam.

6. Serve hot with rice.

elumichampazham rasam
lemon rasam

serves: 4-6
preparation time: 20 minutes
cooking time: 10 minutes

3 tbsp husked green gram
(mung dal)
½ tsp asafoetida powder (hing)
½ tsp turmeric powder
1 tsp salt or to taste
3 tbsp lemon or lime juice

ground to a smooth paste
2-3 green chillies, chopped
½" piece ginger, chopped
1 tbsp water

tempering
2 tsp ghee
1 tsp mustard seeds
½ tsp cumin seeds
¼ tsp black peppercorns,
coarsely crushed
1 dried red chilli, halved
1 sprig curry leaves

garnish
2 tbsp finely chopped coriander
leaves

1. Wash dal and drain. Place dal in a pressure cooker with 1 cup water. Cook under pressure for 5 minutes.

2. Combine dal, asafoetida powder, turmeric powder, salt and 3 cups water in a frying pan. Whisk well. Place pan over low heat and simmer uncovered, stirring occasionally, for 5-7 minutes.

3. Blend in spice paste and simmer for 3-5 minutes, stirring occasionally, till rasam froths up. Remove from heat.

4. Add more water if necessary and simmer once again for 2 minutes.

5. Sprinkle in lemon or lime juice.

6. Heat ghee for tempering in a small pan over moderate heat. Add remaining ingredients for tempering in the order given. When mustard seeds splutter, stir contents of pan into rasam.

7. Garnish with coriander leaves and serve hot with plain rice.

vepampoo rasam
margosa / neem flower rasam

serves: 4-6
soaking time: 10 minutes
preparation time: 10 minutes
cooking time: 15 minutes

3 tsp ghee
1½ tbsp dried margosa flowers
(neem flowers/vepampoo)
1 small lime-sized ball of tamarind
½ tsp rasam powder (page 13)
1 tbsp powdered jaggery
1 medium-sized tomato, quartered
1 tsp salt or to taste

spice paste
1 tsp ghee
1 tsp pigeon peas (tuvar/arhar)
3-4 dried red chillies
½ tsp fenugreek seeds (methi)
½ tsp asafoetida powder (hing)

tempering
2 tsp ghee
1 tsp mustard seeds
1 dried red chilli, halved
1 sprig curry leaves

1. Heat ghee for spice paste in a frying pan over low heat. Add remaining ingredients for spice paste. Fry over low heat, tossing gently, till dal turns golden and chillies and spices are fragrant. Grind to a smooth consistency, gradually adding 2-3 tbsp water.

2. In the same pan, heat 3 tsp ghee and fry margosa flowers till golden. Set aside.

3. Soak tamarind in 1½ cups water for 10 minutes. Extract juice and discard pulp.

4. Combine tamarind juice, rasam powder, jaggery, tomato and salt in a pan. Cover pan and simmer over low heat for 10-12 minutes till the raw aroma of tamarind disappears.

5. Add ½ cup water to spice paste and stir into rasam. Simmer for a couple of minutes, stirring occasionally, till rasam froths up.

6. Add fried margosa flowers and remove from heat.

7. Heat ghee for tempering in a small pan over moderate heat. Add remaining ingredients for tempering in the order given. When mustard seeds splutter, stir contents of pan into rasam.

8. Serve hot with plain rice.

note: Margosa flower rasam is normally prepared during the spring, which is also the season for chicken pox and measles. It is commonly believed that eating margosa flowers prevents these infections.

paruppu rasam
lentil rasam

serves: 4-6
soaking time: 10 minutes
preparation time: 20 minutes
cooking time: 20 minutes

½ cup pigeon peas (tuvar/arhar)

1 medium lime-sized ball of tamarind

½ tsp turmeric powder

2 medium-sized tomatoes, quartered

2 tbsp powdered jaggery

1 tsp salt or to taste

spice paste

1 tbsp coriander seeds

½ tsp mustard seeds

¼ tsp fenugreek seeds (methi)

¾ tsp black peppercorns

¾ tsp cumin seeds

3 tsp oil

2 dried red chillies

½ tsp asafoetida powder (hing)

½ cup grated fresh coconut

tempering

2 tsp ghee

½ tsp mustard seeds

½ tsp cumin seeds

1 dried red chilli, halved

1 sprig curry leaves

garnish

2 tbsp finely chopped coriander leaves

1. Wash dal and drain. Place dal in a pressure cooker with 1 cup water. Cook under pressure for 5 minutes.

2. Soak tamarind in 1½ cups water for 10 minutes. Extract juice and discard pulp.

3. Roast coriander seeds, mustard seeds, fenugreek seeds, peppercorns and cumin seeds for spice paste in a dry frying pan, tossing gently, over low heat till fragrant. Set aside.

4. In the same pan heat oil for spice paste and fry red chillies and asafoetida powder, tossing gently, over low heat till chillies change colour.

5. Combine coconut with all roasted and fried ingredients. Grind to a smooth consistency, gradually adding ¼ cup water.

6. Combine tamarind juice, turmeric powder, tomatoes, jaggery and salt in a frying pan over low heat. Simmer uncovered for 10-12 minutes till the raw aroma of tamarind disappears.

7. Mix in dal and spice paste and simmer for 5-7 minutes, stirring occasionally, till well blended.

8. Add more water if rasam is too thick.

9. Heat ghee for tempering in a small pan over moderate heat and add remaining ingredients for tempering in the order given. When mustard seeds splutter, stir contents of pan into rasam.

10. Garnish with coriander leaves and serve hot with plain rice.

goddu rasam
simple lentil rasam

serves: 4-6
soaking time: 30 minutes
preparation time: 10 minutes
cooking time: 15 minutes

1½ tsp pigeon peas (tuvar/arhar)
1 small lime-sized ball of tamarind
2 tsp rasam powder (page 13)
½ tsp asafoetida powder (hing)
1 tsp salt or to taste

tempering
2 tsp ghee
1 tsp mustard seeds
2 dried red chillies, halved
1 sprig curry leaves

1. Wash dal and soak in ½ cup water for 30 minutes. Drain and grind to a smooth consistency, gradually adding ½ tbsp water.

2. Soak tamarind in 2½ cups water for 10 minutes. Extract juice and discard pulp.

3. Combine tamarind juice, rasam powder, asafoetida powder and salt in a frying pan. Simmer over low heat for 10 minutes till the raw aroma of tamarind disappears.

4. Mix dal paste with 1½ cups water and add to rasam. Simmer for 3-5 minutes, stirring occasionally, till rasam froths up. Remove from heat.

5. Heat ghee for tempering in a small pan over moderate heat. Add remaining ingredients for tempering in the order given. When mustard seeds splutter, stir contents of pan into rasam.

6. Serve hot with plain rice.

killu milagai rasam
chilli rasam

serves: 4-6
soaking time: 10 minutes
preparation time: 10 minutes
cooking time: 50 minutes

¼ cup pigeon peas
(tuvar/arhar – optional)
1 medium lime-sized ball of
tamarind
½ tsp turmeric powder
1 tsp salt or to taste

tempering
3-4 tsp sesame oil (til ka tael)
1 tsp mustard seeds
4-5 round, dried red chillies, halved
½ cup pigeon peas (tuvar/arhar)
¼ tsp fenugreek seeds (methi)
½ tsp asafoetida powder (hing)

garnish
2 tbsp finely chopped coriander
leaves

1. Wash dal (if used) and drain. Place dal in a pressure cooker with 1 cup water. Cook under pressure for 5 minutes.

2. Add 1 cup water to cooked dal, whisk well and set aside.

3. Soak tamarind in 3 cups water for 10 minutes. Extract juice and discard pulp.

4. Heat oil for tempering in a frying pan over low heat. Add remaining ingredients for tempering in the order given. When mustard seeds splutter and dal turns golden, mix in tamarind juice, turmeric powder and salt.

5. Bring to boil, lower heat and simmer for 40-45 minutes, stirring occasionally, till dal is cooked and soft.

6. Mix in cooked dal (if used) and simmer for about 5 minutes, till well blended.

7. Add more water if rasam is too thick.

8. Garnish with coriander leaves.

9. Serve hot with plain rice.

note: The dried red chillies used here are the round variety, not the long ones.

Traditionally, cooked dal is not added to this rasam. It may be added for a thicker consistency.

paruppu urundai rasam
lentil dumpling rasam
You will need an idli rack (described on page 10) to prepare this dish.

serves: 4-6
soaking time: 1 hour
preparation time: 15 minutes
cooking time: 30 minutes

dumplings

¼ cup pigeon peas (tuvar/arhar)

¼ cup husked bengal gram
(chana dal)

3-4 dried red chillies

½ tsp salt or to taste

¼ tsp asafoetida powder (hing)

1 tbsp ghee

1 sprig curry leaves

rasam

1 medium lime-sized ball of
tamarind

3 tsp rasam powder (page 13)

½ tsp asafoetida powder

1 tsp salt or to taste

tempering

2 tsp ghee

1 tsp mustard seeds

1 dried red chilli, halved

½ tsp black peppercorns,
coarsely powdered

1 sprig curry leaves

dumplings

1. Wash dals and soak in 1 cup water with red chillies for 1 hour. Drain dals and mix with salt and asafoetida powder. Grind to a coarse paste, gradually adding 2 tsp water.

2. Heat 1 tbsp ghee in a frying pan. Add curry leaves and fry for a few seconds over low heat. Add dal paste and fry for 1-2 minutes, stirring continuously. Remove from heat.

3. Shape paste into marble-sized balls. Place dumplings in an idli mould and steam for 15 minutes in a pressure cooker (without the weight). Set aside to cool.

rasam

4. Soak tamarind in 3 cups water for 10 minutes. Extract juice and discard pulp.

5. Combine tamarind juice, rasam powder, asafoetida powder and salt in a pan. Place pan over low heat and simmer for 12-15 minutes, till the raw aroma of tamarind disappears.

6. Add more water if necessary.

7. Add dal dumplings and simmer for another 5 minutes. Remove from heat.

8. Heat ghee for tempering in a small pan over moderate heat. Add remaining ingredients for tempering in the order given. When mustard seeds splutter, stir contents of pan into rasam.

9. Serve hot with plain rice.

kosu carrot rasam
cabbage and carrot rasam

serves: 4-6
preparation time: 25 minutes
cooking time: 15 minutes

½ cup pigeon peas (tuvar/arhar)

2 medium-sized tomatoes

1 carrot, finely chopped

½ cup finely chopped cabbage

½ tsp turmeric powder

1 tsp salt or to taste

1½ tbsp lime juice

spice powder

2 tsp oil

1½ tsp black peppercorns

½ tsp cumin seeds

4 tsp coriander seeds

3 tbsp grated dry coconut (copra)

tempering

2 tsp ghee

1 tsp mustard seeds

½ tsp asafoetida powder (hing)

1 dried red chilli, halved

1 sprig curry leaves

garnish

2 tbsp chopped coriander leaves

1. Wash dal and drain. Place dal in a pressure cooker with 1 cup water. Cook under pressure for 5 minutes.

2. Purée tomatoes, strain and set aside.

3. Heat oil for spice powder in a frying pan and add peppercorns, cumin seeds and coriander seeds. Fry over low heat, tossing gently, till fragrant. Stir in copra and remove from heat. Grind to a fine powder and set aside.

4. Bring 2 cups water to a boil in a pan over high heat. Add carrot, cabbage and turmeric powder. Lower heat, cover pan and simmer for 5-7 minutes till vegetables are tender.

5. Stir in cooked dal, tomato purée, salt and spice powder. Add more water if rasam is too thick.

6. Simmer uncovered for 4-5 minutes, stirring occasionally, till well blended. Remove from heat.

7. Heat ghee for tempering in a small pan over moderate heat and add remaining ingredients for tempering. When mustard seeds splutter, stir contents of pan into rasam.

8. Mix in lime juice and garnish with coriander leaves.

9. Serve hot with rice.

paruppu rasam
lentil rasam from chettinad

serves: 4-6
soaking time: 10 minutes
preparation time: 20 minutes
cooking time: 25 minutes

¼ cup pigeon peas (tuvar/arhar)
1 medium lemon-sized ball of tamarind
1½ tsp chettinad rasam podi (page 13)
2 tomatoes, quartered
½ tsp turmeric powder
1 tsp salt or to taste
½ tsp sugar
2 cloves garlic

tempering
2 tsp oil
½ tsp mustard seeds
1 sprig curry leaves

ground to a coarse powder
½ tsp black peppercorns
½ tsp cumin seeds

1. Wash dal and drain. Place dal in a pressure cooker with ½ cup water. Cook under pressure for 5 minutes. Whisk dal and set aside.

2. Soak tamarind in 3 cups water for 10 minutes. Extract juice and discard pulp.

3. Heat oil for tempering in a frying pan over moderate heat. Add remaining ingredients for tempering along with ground spices. When mustard seeds splutter, add rasam powder and stir-fry for 30 seconds.

4. Mix in tamarind juice, tomatoes and turmeric powder. Bring to boil. Lower heat and simmer for 18-20 minutes, stirring occasionally, till the raw aroma of tamarind disappears and rasam is reduced to 2 cups.

5. Add cooked dal and simmer for another 5 minutes, stirring occasionally, and remove from heat.

6. Heat through, if necessary just before serving. Place salt, sugar and garlic in a serving dish. Pour hot rasam over them and serve immediately with plain rice.

note: This rasam cannot be reheated once it has been poured over the salt, sugar and garlic.

cobbari paala pappucharu
coconut milk and lentil rasam from andhra pradesh

serves: 4-6
preparation time: 30 minutes
cooking time: 25 minutes

1 cup pigeon peas (tuvar/arhar)
2½ cups grated coconut
1 cup shallots, peeled and kept whole
4-5 green chillies, finely chopped
1" piece ginger, grated
½ tsp turmeric powder
1½ tsp salt or to taste
1½ tbsp lime juice

tempering
2 tsp oil
1 tsp mustard seeds
1 tsp cumin seeds
½ tsp asafoetida powder (hing)
3-4 cloves garlic (optional)
1 dried red chilli, halved
1 sprig curry leaves

garnish
2 tbsp chopped coriander leaves

1. Wash dal and drain. Place dal in a pressure cooker with 2 cups water and cook under pressure for 5 minutes.

2. Mix grated coconut with 2 cups hot water. Process for 1-2 minutes in a blender. Pour liquid through a strainer lined with muslin cloth and press out thick coconut milk.

3. Add 1½ cups hot water to coconut residue. Blend and strain once more to extract thin coconut milk.

4. Mix thin coconut milk with thick milk in a heavy-based pan and pour in cooked dal. Whisk till well blended.

5. Add shallots, green chillies, ginger, turmeric powder and salt to pan and mix well.

6. Place pan on high heat and bring to boil, stirring continuously. Lower heat and simmer for 20-25 minutes, stirring frequently, till shallots are tender.

7. Heat oil for tempering in a small pan over moderate heat. Add remaining ingredients for tempering in the order given. When mustard seeds splutter, stir contents of pan into rasam.

8. Remove from heat and mix in lime juice.

9. Garnish with coriander leaves and serve hot with rice.

bellay saaru
lentil rasam from karnataka

serves: 4-6
soaking time: 10 minutes
preparation time: 20 minutes
cooking time: 30 minutes

¼ cup pigeon peas (tuvar/arhar)

1 lemon-sized ball of tamarind

2 tomatoes, chopped

2 green chillies, finely chopped

1 tbsp + 1 tbsp chopped coriander leaves

1 sprig curry leaves

1 tsp salt or to taste

½ tsp turmeric powder

spice powder
1 tbsp oil

3-4 tbsp pigeon peas (tuvar/arhar)

4 dried red chillies

1 tsp cumin seeds

1 tsp fenugreek seeds (methi)

½ tsp mustard seeds

½ tsp asafoetida powder (hing)

¼ tsp black peppercorns

4-5 cloves garlic (optional)

tempering
2 tsp ghee

½ tsp mustard seeds

¼ tsp asafoetida powder

1 dried red chilli, halved

1 sprig curry leaves

1. Wash dal and drain. Place dal in a pressure cooker with ½ cup water and cook under pressure for 5 minutes. Whisk dal and set aside.

2. Heat oil for spice powder in a frying pan. Add remaining ingredients for spice powder. Fry over low heat, tossing gently, till dal turns golden and chillies and spices are fragrant. Cool and grind to a fine powder.

3. Soak tamarind in 3 cups water. Extract juice and discard pulp.

4. Pour tamarind juice into a pan and add tomatoes. Squash tomatoes roughly. Add whisked dal, green chillies, 1 tbsp coriander leaves, curry leaves and salt. Mix well, place pan over high heat and bring to boil. Lower heat and simmer for 20-22 minutes, stirring occasionally.

5. Mix in turmeric powder and spice powder, and simmer for 3-5 minutes, stirring occasionally.

6. Heat ghee for tempering in a small pan over moderate heat. Add remaining ingredients for tempering in the order given. When mustard seeds splutter, stir contents of pan into saaru.

7. Garnish with remaining coriander leaves.

8. Serve hot with plain rice.

nellikai rasam
amla rasam

serves: 4-6
preparation time: 15 minutes
cooking time: 20 minutes

¼ cup pigeon peas (tuvar/arhar)
*¼ cup husked bengal gram
(chana dal)*
*1 cup (250 gms) chopped amla
(see note alongside)*
½" piece ginger, grated
3-4 green chillies, finely chopped
2 sprigs curry leaves
1 tsp salt or to taste

tempering
2 tsp coconut oil
½ tsp mustard seeds
1 dried red chilli, halved
1 sprig curry leaves

1. Wash dals and drain. Place dals in a pressure cooker with 2 cups water and cook under pressure for 5 minutes.

2. Add 2 cups water to cooked dal in a pan and whisk well.

3. Mix in amla, ginger, green chillies, curry leaves and salt. Bring to boil, lower heat and simmer for at least 18-20 minutes, stirring occasionally, till amla is tender.

4. If rasam is too thick, add 1 cup water and simmer for another 2-3 minutes.

5. Heat oil for tempering in a small pan over moderate heat. Add remaining ingredients for tempering in the order given. When mustard seeds splutter, stir contents of pan into rasam.

6. Serve hot with rice.

note: The botanical name for amla is Emblica officinalis. It is a jade-green, tart fruit also known as the emblic gooseberry or Indian hog plum.

poriyal & kootu

yengai kathirikai kariamudhu
curried aubergine from the hebbar iyengar community of karnataka

serves: 4-6
soaking time: 10 minutes
preparation time: 20 minutes
cooking time: 20 minutes

1 small marble-sized ball of tamarind
20-22 (500 gms) small aubergines (baingan) cut into 1" lengths
½ tsp turmeric powder
1 tsp salt or to taste
2 tsp grated dry coconut (copra)

spice powder
1½ tbsp husked bengal gram (chana dal)
1½ tbsp husked black gram (urad dal)
2 dried red chillies
3 tbsp coriander seeds
½" stick cinnamon
1 clove
1 marathi moggu (optional - see note alongside)

tempering
2 tbsp oil
1 tsp mustard seeds
1 tsp husked black gram (urad dal)
1 tsp husked bengal gram (chana dal)
1 dried red chilli, halved
1 sprig curry leaves

1. Soak tamarind in ¼ cup water for 10 minutes. Extract juice and discard pulp.

2. Combine all ingredients for spice powder in a dry frying pan over low heat. Toss gently, till dals are golden and chillies and spices are fragrant. Cool and grind to a fine powder.

3. Heat oil for tempering in a heavy-based frying pan over moderate heat. Add all ingredients for tempering in the order given. When mustard seeds splutter, add aubergines and sauté, stirring occasionally, for 2-3 minutes. Mix in tamarind juice, turmeric powder and salt.

4. Cover pan and simmer over low heat, stirring occasionally, till aubergines are tender. If necessary, sprinkle in a little water.

5. When aubergines are tender and all liquid absorbed, sprinkle in copra and spice powder. Give it a stir and remove from heat.

6. Serve hot as a side dish.

note: Marathi moggu is a spice resembling a large clove that is commonly used in Karnataka cuisine.

*Right : Guthi bendakai
(Stuffed okra from Andhra Pradesh) see page 72*

vazhakkai masala poriyal
curried green plantain

serves: 4-6
preparation time: 10 minutes
cooking time: 20 minutes

½ tsp turmeric powder

1 tsp salt or to taste

3 cups (2 medium-sized) peeled and sliced (½" slices) unripe green plantains

1 medium-sized onion, finely chopped (optional)

ground to a paste

4 dried red chillies

1 tsp coriander seeds

1 tsp roasted Bengal gram (bhuna chana)

½" stick cinnamon

½ tsp poppy seeds (khus-khus), powdered

2 tsp water

tempering

3 tsp oil

½ tsp mustard seeds

½ tsp cumin seeds

1 tsp husked black gram (urad dal)

¼ tsp asafoetida powder (hing)

1 sprig curry leaves

1. Heat 1 cup water in a pan. Sprinkle in turmeric powder and salt and bring to boil over high heat. Add plantains, lower heat and simmer for 7-8 minutes, till tender. Drain well. Set aside to cool.

2. Smear ground paste evenly over plantains.

3. Heat oil for tempering in a frying pan over moderate heat. Add remaining ingredients for tempering in the order given. When mustard seeds splutter, add onion and fry till golden.

4. Mix in plantains and fry for 1-2 minutes, stirring frequently, till well blended.

5. Remove from heat and serve as a side dish.

Left : Kosu pattani poricha kootu
(Cabbage and green peas stew from Thirunelveli) see page 77

carrot poriyal
carrot with coconut from tamil nadu

serves: 4-6
soaking time: 10 minutes
preparation time: 15 minutes
cooking time: 10 minutes

2 tbsp husked green gram
(mung dal)
½ kg carrot, finely chopped
¼ tsp turmeric powder
1 tsp salt or to taste

ground to a coarse paste
6 tbsp grated fresh coconut
1-2 green chillies
1 tsp cumin seeds
1½ tbsp water

tempering
2 tsp ghee
½ tsp mustard seeds
1 tsp husked black gram
(urad dal)
¼ tsp asafoetida powder (hing)
1 dried red chilli, halved
1 sprig curry leaves

1. Wash dal and soak in ½ cup water for 10 minutes. Heat ghee for tempering in a frying pan over moderate heat. Add remaining ingredients for tempering in the order given. When mustard seeds splutter, drain dal and add to pan with carrot, turmeric powder, salt and 1 cup water.

2. Cover pan and cook on high heat for 5-7 minutes, stirring occasionally, till carrot is tender and water is absorbed.

3. Add ground paste, mix till well blended and remove from heat.

4. Serve hot as a side dish.

kudamilagai poriyal
stir-fried capsicum

serves: 4-6
preparation time: 10 minutes
cooking time: 15 minutes

4-5 (500 gms) medium-sized
capsicums, cut into ¼" squares
3 tbsp gram flour (besan)
3 tbsp oil
2 tsp coriander powder
½ tsp red chilli powder
½ tsp asafoetida powder (hing)
1 tsp salt or to taste

tempering
2 tsp oil
1 tsp mustard seeds
1 tsp cumin seeds
1 dried red chilli, halved
1 sprig curry leaves

1. Heat oil for tempering in a frying pan over moderate heat. Add remaining ingredients for tempering in the order given. When mustard seeds splutter, add capsicums and sauté for 1-2 minutes.

2. Sprinkle in 2 tbsp water, lower heat, cover pan and simmer for 2 minutes.

3. Combine gram flour, oil, coriander powder, chilli powder, asafoetida powder and salt in a bowl.

4. Add to capsicums and stir-fry over low heat for 5-7 minutes till capsicums are tender and the raw aroma of gram flour disappears.

5. The poriyal should be completely dry.

6. Serve hot as a side dish.

urulaikizhangu poriyal
stir-fried potato with coconut

serves: 4-6
preparation time: 20 minutes
cooking time: 10 minutes

5-6 (500 gms) medium-sized
potatoes

½ tsp turmeric powder

½ tsp red chilli powder

1 green chilli, slit lengthwise

1 tsp salt or to taste

3-4 tbsp grated fresh coconut

tempering

1 tbsp oil

1 tsp mustard seeds

1 tsp cumin seeds

1 tsp husked black gram
(urad dal)

1 tsp husked bengal gram
(chana dal)

½ tsp asafoetida powder (hing)

1 dried red chilli, halved

1 sprig curry leaves

1. Boil potatoes in their jackets. Peel and cut into ½" cubes.

2. Heat oil for tempering in a frying pan over moderate heat. Add remaining ingredients for tempering in the order given. When mustard seeds splutter, add potatoes, turmeric powder, chilli powder, green chilli and salt. Stir-fry for 1-2 minutes over low heat till potatoes are well coated with spices.

3. Sprinkle in coconut and mix till well blended.

4. Serve hot as a side dish.

vankai battani aava kura
aubergine and green peas in a mustard sauce from andhra pradesh

serves: 4-6
soaking time: 10 minutes
preparation time: 20 minutes
cooking time: 15 minutes

20-22 (500 gms) small aubergines (baingan)
1 cup curd whisked with 3 cups water
1 marble-sized ball of tamarind
½ cup shelled green peas
½" piece ginger, grated
1 tsp salt or to taste

ground to a paste
1 tsp mustard seeds
2 tsp white sesame seeds (til)
2 dried red chillies
2 tsp rice flour
1-2 tbsp water

tempering
2 tsp oil
¼ tsp fenugreek seeds (methi)
1 tsp mustard seeds
2 dried red chillies, halved
1 tsp husked black gram (urad dal)
½ tsp asafoetida powder (hing)
1 sprig curry leaves

1. Quarter aubergines and soak in diluted curd to prevent discolouring.

2. Soak tamarind in ½ cup water. Extract juice and discard pulp.

3. Drain aubergines and place in a pan with green peas and ½ cup water. Simmer covered over low heat for 5-7 minutes, till vegetables are cooked and water is completely absorbed.

4. Heat oil for tempering in a frying pan over moderate heat. Add remaining ingredients for tempering in the order given. When mustard seeds splutter, add tamarind juice, ginger and salt.

5. Simmer over low heat for 8-10 minutes, till the raw aroma of tamarind disappears.

6. Add ground paste and simmer for a minute, stirring frequently. Add aubergines and green peas.

7. Cook over low heat, stirring frequently, till well blended.

8. The vegetables should be completely dry. Serve as a side dish.

variation: You can substitute cluster beans for aubergines. It will taste equally delicious.

murungakeerai poriyal
drumstick leaves with lentils and coconut

serves: 4-6
preparation time: 20 minutes
cooking time: 35 minutes

¼ cup pigeon peas (tuvar/arhar)
3 cups drumstick leaves, finely chopped
1 tsp sugar
¾ tsp salt or to taste
3 tbsp grated fresh coconut

tempering
2 tsp oil
½ tsp mustard seeds
½ tsp cumin seeds
1 tsp husked black gram (urad dal)
1 dried red chilli, halved

1. Wash dal and drain. Place dal in a pan with 1½ cups water over low heat. Simmer for 30-40 minutes, till cooked. Strain out excess water and reserve dal.

2. Heat oil for tempering in a frying pan over moderate heat. Add remaining ingredients for tempering in the order given. When mustard seeds splutter, add drumstick leaves, sugar, salt and ¼ cup water.

3. Cover pan and cook over low heat for 5-7 minutes, stirring occasionally, till leaves are tender and water is absorbed.

4. Stir in cooked dal and grated coconut.

5. Serve as a side dish.

pudalangai poriyal
snake gourd with lentils from kongunadu

serves: 4-6
soaking time: 1 hour
preparation time: 10 minutes
cooking time: 10 minutes

2 tbsp pigeon peas (tuvar/arhar)
2 tbsp husked bengal gram (chana dal)
500 gms snake gourd (chirchinda)
1 tsp salt or to taste
4 tbsp grated fresh coconut

tempering
2 tsp oil
1 tsp mustard seeds
1 tsp husked black gram (urad dal)
1 dried red chilli, halved
¼ tsp asafoetida powder (hing)
1 sprig curry leaves

1. Combine dals and wash. Drain and soak in water for 1 hour.

2. Chop off the ends of snake gourd and discard. Cut snake gourd in half lengthwise. Remove and discard seeds. Cut snake gourd into fine slices.

3. Heat oil for tempering in a frying pan over moderate heat. Add remaining ingredients for tempering in the order given. When mustard seeds splutter, drain dals and add to pan with snake gourd, salt and 1 cup water.

4. Cover pan and cook over high heat for 7-9 minutes, stirring occasionally, till gourd and dals are tender and moisture is completely absorbed.

5. Remove from heat and sprinkle in coconut.

6. Mix well and serve as a side dish.

urulaikizhangu poriyal
stir-fried potatoes from thirunelveli

serves: 4-6
preparation time: 25 minutes
cooking time: 10 minutes

8-9 (1 kg) medium-sized potatoes
1 tsp salt or to taste
1½ tbsp gram flour (besan)

ground to a paste
3 onions, roughly chopped
4 dried red chillies

tempering
2 tsp oil
1 tsp mustard seeds
1 tsp husked black gram (urad dal)
1 dried red chilli, halved
1 sprig curry leaves

garnish
2 tbsp finely chopped coriander leaves

1. Boil potatoes in their jackets. Peel and cut into ¼" cubes.

2. Heat oil for tempering in a frying pan over moderate heat. Add remaining ingredients for tempering in the order given. When mustard seeds splutter, add ground paste and sauté for 2-3 minutes.

3. Add potatoes and salt. Stir-fry for 1-2 minutes.

4. Sprinkle in gram flour and continue stir-frying for 3-4 minutes, till the raw aroma of gram flour disappears.

5. Garnish with coriander leaves and serve hot as a side dish.

beetroot parupu usili
stir-fried beetroot with lentil crumble from chettinad

serves: 4-6
soaking time: 1 hour
preparation time: 30 minutes
cooking time: 30 minutes

½ cup pigeon peas (tuvar/arhar)
½ cup husked bengal gram (chana dal)
6 dried red chillies
½ tsp asafoetida powder (hing)
¾ tsp + ¾ tsp salt or to taste
4 cups (500 gms) grated beetroot
1 onion, finely chopped

tempering
3 tbsp oil
1 tsp mustard seeds
1 tsp husked black gram (urad dal)
1 dried red chilli, halved
1 sprig curry leaves

1. Wash dals and soak in 2 cups water with red chillies for 1 hour. Drain and grind to a coarse batter, gradually adding ⅓-½ cup water.

2. Add asafoetida powder and ¾ tsp salt. Mix well and set aside.

3. Place beetroot in a frying pan with ¾ tsp salt and ½ cup water over low heat. Cover pan and cook for 7-9 minutes, stirring occasionally, till tender. Transfer beetroot to a bowl and set aside.

4. In the same pan, heat oil for tempering over moderate heat. Add remaining ingredients for tempering in the order given. When mustard seeds splutter, add onion and fry till pink.

5. Blend in dal batter and fry over low heat stirring frequently, till mixture is well cooked, crisp and resembles breadcrumbs (but not hard).

6. Mix in beetroot and stir-fry for 5 minutes till well blended.

7. Serve hot as a side dish.

idichakka thoran
stir-fried tender jackfruit with coconut from kerala

serves: 4-6
preparation time: 20 minutes
cooking time: 20 minutes

3 cups roughly chopped tender jackfruit (see note alongside)
¼ tsp turmeric powder
1 tsp salt or to taste

ground to a coarse paste
1 cup grated fresh coconut
¼ tsp cumin seeds
½ tsp red chilli powder
2 cloves garlic (optional)
2-3 tbsp water

tempering
2 tbsp coconut oil
½ tsp mustard seeds
1 tsp rice grains
2 dried red chillies, halved
1 sprig curry leaves

1. Place jackfruit in a pan with turmeric powder, salt and 1 cup water. Cook over low heat for 10-12 minutes, till tender. Drain and crush jackfruit with a ladle into small shreds.

2. Blend in ground paste and set aside.

3. Heat oil for tempering in a frying pan over moderate heat. Add remaining ingredients for tempering in the order given. When mustard seeds splutter, add jackfruit.

4. Stir-fry for 3-4 minutes till mixture is dry.

5. Serve hot as a side dish.

note: You would need to buy at least 500 gms of tender jackfruit to get 3 cups of cleaned and chopped jackfruit.

urulaikizhangu podi
potato crumble from tamil nadu

serves: 4-6
preparation time: 20 minutes
cooking time: 5 minutes

3 medium-sized potatoes
¼ tsp + ½ tsp salt or to taste

spice powder
1 tbsp oil
2 tbsp husked bengal gram (chana dal)
2 tbsp husked black gram (urad dal)
1 tbsp pigeon peas (arhar/tuvar)
6 dried red chillies
½ tsp asafoetida powder (hing)

1. Boil potatoes in their jackets, peel and grate. Set aside.

2. Heat oil for spice powder in a wok/frying pan over moderate heat. Add remaining ingredients for spice powder and fry over low heat. Toss gently, till dals turn golden and chillies and spices are fragrant. Mix with ¼ tsp salt and grind to a fine powder.

3. Return spice powder to pan. Blend in potato and ½ tsp salt.

4. Place pan on low heat and cook for 2-3 minutes, stirring continuously, till well blended.

5. Serve with rice as a side dish

note: It can also be served mixed with rice and a tsp of ghee.

pudalangai pooranam
stuffed snake gourd

serves: 4-6
preparation time: 20 minutes
cooking time: 20 minutes

*a one-foot-long tender snake
gourd (chirchinda)*
1 tbsp lime juice
¾ tsp salt or to taste
2 tbsp oil

ground to a smooth paste
¾ cup grated fresh coconut
3-4 green chillies
2 tsp cumin seeds
2 tbsp chopped coriander leaves
¼ cup water

tempering
2 tsp oil
½ tsp mustard seeds
1 dried red chilli, halved
1 sprig curry leaves

1. Chop off and discard both ends of snake gourd. Slice snake gourd into 1" pieces, without peeling it. Scoop out seeds from within the slices to make hollow cylinders. Set aside.

2. Mix spice paste with lime juice and half the salt.

3. Heat oil for tempering in a pan over moderate heat. Add remaining ingredients for tempering in the order given. When mustard seeds splutter, add spice paste and fry over low heat for 1-2 minutes, stirring continuously.

4. Remove pan from heat. Cool and stuff snake gourd cylinders with spices.

5. Place a frying pan over moderate heat and add 2 tbsp oil. Add stuffed snake gourd, sprinkle with a little water, and cook over low heat for 8-10 minutes, till tender. Stir gently, taking care not to break them.

6. Serve hot as a side dish with rice or roti.

guthi bendakai
stuffed okra from andhra pradesh

serves: 4-6
preparation time: 20 minutes
cooking time: 20 minutes

500 gms small, tender okra
(bhindi)
1 tsp salt
½ tsp turmeric powder

spice powder
2 tsp oil
5 dried red chillies
2½ tsp cumin seeds
2 sprigs curry leaves

tempering
1 tbsp oil
½ tsp mustard seeds
1 tsp husked black gram (urad dal)
1 dried red chilli, halved

1. Wash okra and dry thoroughly. Make a slit lengthwise, at the tail end, coming three-quarters of the way up, ensuring that the segments do not separate.

2. Heat oil for spice powder in a pan over moderate heat. Add remaining ingredients for spice powder and fry over low heat, tossing gently, till fragrant.

3. Cool and add salt and turmeric powder. Grind to a fine powder.

4. Stuff okra with spice powder and set aside.

5. Heat oil for tempering in a pan over moderate heat. Add remaining ingredients for tempering in the order given. When mustard seeds splutter, add okra and sauté gently for 1-2 minutes.

6. Lower heat, cover pan and cook for 10-12 minutes, stirring occasionally till okra are tender. Taste and add more salt if necessary.

7. Serve hot as a side dish.

senai urundai
yam fritters from kongunadu

serves: 4-6
preparation time: 20 minutes
cooking time: 20 minutes

1¾ cups grated yam (see note alongside)

4-5 dried red chillies

½ cup roasted peanuts

1¼ cups grated fresh coconut

1 tsp fennel seeds (saunf)

½ tsp turmeric powder

¼ cup gram flour (besan)

2 medium-sized onions, finely chopped

1 sprig curry leaves

2 tbsp chopped coriander leaves

1 tsp salt or to taste

oil for deep frying

1. Combine yam, red chillies, peanuts, coconut, fennel seeds and turmeric powder in a bowl. Grind to a coarse paste resembling vadai batter, gradually adding ½ cup water.

2. Add gram flour, onions, curry leaves, coriander leaves and salt to yam paste. Mix well.

3. Heat oil in a deep frying pan to smoking point. Drop spoonfuls of batter into hot oil. Lower heat to moderate and fry fritters in batches, turning frequently, till golden brown and crisp.

4. Drain and place on kitchen paper to absorb excess oil.

5. Serve as a side dish or a teatime snack.

note: *You need to buy about 400 gms of yam to get 1¾ cups of the cleaned and grated vegetable.*

kathirikai kootu
aubergine stew

serves: 4-6
preparation time: 30 minutes
cooking time: 20 minutes

½ cup pigeon peas (arhar/tuvar)
½ tsp turmeric powder
2 tsp oil
½ cup raw peanuts, with skin
500 gms small aubergines
(baingan), cubed and soaked in
water
1 tsp salt or to taste

spice paste
2-3 dried red chillies
1½ tsp coriander seeds
½ tsp asafoetida powder (hing)
1 tsp oil
3-4 tbsp grated fresh coconut

tempering
1 tsp oil
½ tsp mustard seeds
½ tsp husked bengal gram
(chana dal)
1 sprig curry leaves

1. Wash dal and drain. Place dal in a pressure cooker with turmeric powder and 1 cup water. Cook under pressure for 5 minutes.

2. Combine red chillies, coriander seeds, and asafoetida powder for spice paste in a dry frying pan. Place pan over low heat and roast, tossing gently, till chillies and spices are fragrant. Remove from pan and set aside.

3. In the same pan heat oil for spice paste over low heat and fry coconut till golden.

4. Combine all ingredients for spice paste, and grind to a smooth consistency, gradually adding ¼ cup water.

5. Heat 2 tsp oil in the same pan over moderate heat. Add peanuts and toss for 1-2 minutes.

6. Drain aubergines and add to pan with salt and 1 cup water.

7. Simmer over low heat, stirring occasionally for 10-12 minutes, till aubergines are tender.

8. Mix in cooked dal and spice paste. Simmer for 7-8 minutes, stirring occasionally, till well blended.

9. Heat oil for tempering in a small pan over moderate heat. Add remaining ingredients for tempering in the order given. When mustard seeds splutter, stir contents of pan into kootu.

10. Serve hot with rice or as a side dish.

kaikari milagu kootu
pepper-flavoured vegetable stew

serves: 4-6
preparation time: 30 minutes
cooking time: 20 minutes

*½ cup husked green gram
(mung dal)*
1½ cups grated fresh coconut
2 tsp rice flour
2 tomatoes, quartered
*1 cup finely chopped choko
(chow chow)*
1½ cups cauliflower florets
½ cup shelled green peas
1 tsp salt or to taste
½ tsp turmeric powder

spice powder
1 tsp ghee
1 tsp black peppercorns
1 tbsp coriander seed
½ tsp asafoetida powder (hing)

tempering
2 tsp ghee
1 tsp mustard seeds
1 sprig curry leaves

1. Roast dal in a dry frying pan over low heat till fragrant. Wash well and drain. Place dal in a pressure cooker with 1 cup water. Cook under pressure for 5 minutes.

2. Mix grated coconut with 1 cup hot water. Process for 1-2 minutes in a blender. Pour liquid through a strainer lined with muslin cloth and press out thick coconut milk. Blend in rice flour and set aside.

3. Heat ghee for spice powder in a frying pan over moderate heat. Add remaining ingredients for spice powder. Fry over low heat, tossing gently, till fragrant. Cool and grind to a fine powder.

4. Heat ghee for tempering in the same pan over moderate heat. Add mustard seeds and curry leaves. When mustard seeds splutter, add tomatoes and stir-fry for 1-2 minutes.

5. Add remaining vegetables and toss gently. Stir in salt, turmeric powder and 1 cup water.

6. Simmer for 8-10 minutes, stirring occasionally till vegetables are tender.

7. Blend in dal and spice powder and cook for 1-2 minutes.

8. Pour in coconut milk and simmer for a minute, stirring continuously.

9. Remove from heat and serve hot with rice or roti.

vazhakkai milagu kootu
green plantain and pepper stew

serves: 4-6
preparation time: 20 minutes
cooking time: 15 minutes

1¼ cups grated fresh coconut

½ cup curd

3 medium-sized green plantains

1 tsp salt or to taste

spice paste

2 tsp husked bengal gram
(chana dal)

2 tsp wheat grains (gehun)

2 dried red chillies

½ tsp black peppercorns

1 tsp coriander seeds

¼ tsp fenugreek seeds (methi)

½ tsp rice grains

½ tsp asafoetida powder (hing)

tempering

2 tsp ghee

1 tsp mustard seeds

1 sprig curry leaves

1. Combine all ingredients for spice paste and roast in a dry frying pan over low heat. Toss gently, till dal turns golden and chillies and spices are fragrant.

2. Add coconut and grind to a smooth paste, gradually adding ½ cup water.

3. Add spice paste to curd and whisk till well blended and smooth. Set aside.

4. Peel plantains and cut into ¼" cubes.

5. Place 1½ cups water in a pan over high heat and bring to boil. Add plantains and simmer over moderate heat for 5-7 minutes, till tender.

6. Blend in spiced curd and salt and simmer over low heat, stirring occasionally, for 1-2 minutes. Mix in ½ cup extra water if required and simmer for an additional 1-2 minutes.

7. Heat ghee for tempering in a small pan over moderate heat. Add mustard seeds and curry leaves. When mustard seeds splutter, stir contents of pan into milagu kootu.

8. Serve hot with rice or as a side dish.

*Right : Urulaikizhangu kurma
(Curried potatoes from Chettinad) see page 82*

kosu-pattani poricha kootu
cabbage and green pea stew
from thirunelveli

serves: 4-6
preparation time: 25 minutes
cooking time: 15 minutes

¼ cup husked green gram
(mung dal)
5 cups (500 gms) finely chopped
cabbage
¾ cup shelled green peas
1 carrot, finely chopped
½ tsp turmeric powder
1 tsp salt or to taste

ground to a smooth paste
4-5 dried red chillies
2 tsp cumin seeds
¾ cup grated fresh coconut
½ cup water

tempering
2 tsp oil
1 tsp mustard seeds
1 tsp husked black gram (urad dal)
1 sprig curry leaves

1. Wash dal and drain. Place dal in a pressure cooker with ½ cup water. Cook under pressure for 3 minutes

2. Heat 1½ cups water in a pan over moderate heat. Add cabbage, green peas, carrot, turmeric and salt. Simmer for 8-10 minutes, till vegetables are tender.

3. Blend in ground paste and dal. Simmer for 5 minutes, stirring occasionally.

4. Heat oil for tempering in a small pan over moderate heat. Add remaining ingredients for tempering in the order given. When mustard seeds splutter, stir contents of pan into kootu.

5. Serve hot with plain rice or roti.

Left : Senai urundai
(Yam fritters from Kongunadu) see page 73

pooshinikai kootu
ash gourd stew from north arcot

serves: 4-6
soaking time: 30 minutes
preparation time: 30 minutes
cooking time: 20 minutes

½ cup pigeon peas (tuvar/arhar)

1 medium lemon-sized ball of tamarind

2½ cups (750 gms) peeled and chopped (½" cubes) ash gourd (petha)

½ cup raw peanuts

1 tsp salt or to taste

spice paste

2 tsp oil

1 tsp husked bengal gram (chana dal)

1 tsp coriander seeds

½ tsp asafoetida powder (hing)

3-4 dried red chillies

¾ cup grated fresh coconut

tempering

2 tsp oil

¾ tsp mustard seeds

1 dried red chilli, halved

1 sprig curry leaves

1. Wash dal and drain. Place dal in a pressure cooker with 1 cup water and cook under pressure for 5 minutes.

2. Soak tamarind in 1 cup water for 10 minutes. Extract juice and discard pulp.

3. Soak peanuts in water for 30 minutes. Drain and set aside.

4. Heat oil for spice paste in a frying pan over moderate heat. Add all ingredients for spice paste, except coconut and fry over low heat. Toss gently, till dal turns golden.

5. Remove from heat. Mix in coconut and grind to a smooth paste, gradually adding ½ cup water.

6. Combine tamarind juice, ash gourd, peanuts and salt in the same frying pan and place over low heat. Simmer for at least 10-12 minutes till the raw aroma of tamarind disappears.

7. Stir in dal and spice paste. Simmer uncovered for about 5 minutes, stirring occasionally, till well blended.

8. Heat oil for tempering in a small pan. Add remaining ingredients for tempering in the order given. When mustard seeds splutter, stir contents of pan into kootu.

9. Serve hot with plain rice or roti.

moru keerai
amaranth in curd

serves: 4-6
preparation time: 10 minutes
cooking time: 15 minutes

1¼ cups fresh curd
1 tsp salt or to taste
4 cups tightly packed amaranth greens, finely chopped

spice paste
1 tsp oil
1 dried red chilli
1 green chilli
¾ tsp cumin seeds
½ tsp asafoetida powder
½ tsp rice grains
4 tbsp coconut, grated

tempering
2 tsp ghee
1 tsp mustard seeds
1 tsp cumin seeds
1 tsp husked black gram (urad dal)
1 dried red chilli, halved
1 sprig curry leaves

1. Heat oil for spice paste in a frying pan over moderate heat. Add remaining ingredients for spice paste and fry over low heat, tossing gently, till chillies and spices are fragrant. Grind to a smooth consistency, gradually adding 2 tbsp water.

2. Combine curd, salt and spice paste in a bowl and whisk till well blended and smooth.

3. Heat ½ cup water in the same frying pan. Add amaranth leaves. Cover pan and simmer for 5-7 minutes, till tender.

4. Remove pan from heat. With the back of a ladle, lightly mash amaranth leaves.

5. Add spiced curd to pan and return to low heat. Simmer for 5 minutes, stirring continuously, till well blended.

6. Heat ghee for tempering in a small frying pan over moderate heat. Add remaining ingredients for tempering in the order given. When mustard seeds splutter, stir contents of pan into moru keerai.

7. Serve hot as a side dish.

alu gaddé song
curried potatoes from mangalore

serves: 4
preparation time: 20 minutes
cooking time: 15 minutes

4 medium-sized potatoes

3-4 tbsp coconut oil

1 sprig curry leaves

2 medium-sized onions, finely chopped

1 tsp salt or to taste

spice paste

1 tsp oil

4 dried red chillies

¼ tsp fenugreek seeds (methi)

½ tsp turmeric powder

1 cup grated fresh coconut

1 marble-sized ball of tamarind, without seeds or strings

1. Boil potatoes in their jackets. Peel and cut into ½" cubes.

2. Heat oil for spice paste in a wok/frying pan over moderate heat. Add red chillies and fenugreek seeds, Fry over low heat, till fenugreek seeds are fragrant and golden.

3. Combine fried ingredients with remaining ingredients for spice paste and grind to a smooth consistency, gradually adding ¼ cup water.

4. Heat coconut oil in the same wok/frying pan over moderate heat. Add curry leaves and onions. Sauté for about 4-5 minutes till onions are golden.

5. Blend in spice paste and sauté for 1-2 minutes.

6. Add potatoes, salt and ¾-1 cup water. Simmer for 5-7 minutes, stirring frequently, till well blended.

7. Serve hot as a side dish with rice or roti.

bangala dumpa kurma
potato curry from andhra pradesh

serves: 3-4
preparation time: 20 minutes
cooking time: 20 minutes

3-4 medium-sized potatoes

oil for deep frying

1 sprig curry leaves

2 medium-sized onions, finely sliced

1 green chilli, halved lengthwise

1 tsp red chilli powder

½ tsp turmeric powder

¾ tsp salt or to taste

¼ cup milk

ground to a smooth paste

1 green cardamom

1 clove

½" stick cinnamon

½ tsp poppy seeds (khus-khus), powdered

1 tsp coriander seeds

½" piece ginger, grated

2 cloves garlic (optional)

2-3 tbsp water

garnish

2 tbsp finely chopped coriander leaves

1. Wash potatoes, peel and cut into 1" cubes.

2. Heat oil for deep frying in a wok/deep frying pan over moderate heat. Fry potatoes till golden. Drain and set aside.

3. Heat 2 tbsp of the same oil in a frying pan over moderate heat. Add curry leaves, onions and green chilli. Sauté till onions are golden.

4. Add potatoes, chilli powder, turmeric powder, salt and ½ cup water. Cover pan and simmer for 8-10 minutes, stirring occasionally, till water is completely absorbed and potatoes are tender.

5. Blend in milk and spice paste. Simmer uncovered for another 5-7 minutes, stirring continuously, till well blended.

6. Garnish with coriander leaves and serve hot with roti or plain rice.

urulaikizhangu kurma
curried potatoes from chettinad

serves: 4-6
soaking time: 30 minutes
preparation time: 30 minutes
cooking time: 25 minutes

1 kg potatoes
2-3 tbsp ghee
1 bay leaf
2-3 cloves
1" stick cinnamon
3 medium-sized onions, finely chopped
½ tsp turmeric powder
1¼ tsp salt or to taste
1 sprig curry leaves

spice paste
6-8 cashew nuts
1 tbsp oil
1 tbsp poppy seeds (powdered)
2 tsp coriander seeds
1 tbsp fennel seeds (saunf)
5-6 dried red chillies
2 tsp roasted Bengal gram (bhuna chana)
1" piece ginger, finely chopped
3-4 tbsp grated fresh cocoanut

garnish
2 tbsp finely chopped coriander leaves

1. Wash potatoes, peel and cut into ½" cubes.

2. Soak cashew nuts for spice paste in ½ cup warm water for 30 minutes. Drain well and set aside.

3. Heat oil for spice paste in a frying pan over moderate heat. Add poppy seeds, coriander seeds, fennel seeds and red chillies and fry, tossing gently, till fragrant.

4. Remove from heat and mix in cashew nuts and remaining ingredients for spice paste. Grind to a smooth consistency, gradually adding ¼ cup water.

5. Heat ghee in a wok/frying pan over moderate heat. Add bay leaf, cloves and cinnamon and toss for a minute.

6. Add onions and fry till golden.

7. Blend in spice paste and fry for 3-4 minutes over low heat, stirring continuously.

8. Mix in potatoes, turmeric powder, salt, curry leaves and 2 cups water. Simmer for at least 10-12 minutes, stirring frequently, till potatoes are tender. Add ½ cup water if kurma is too thick.

9. Garnish with coriander leaves and serve hot with roti, paratha or puri.

note: Instead of simmering the potatoes, they can be cooked under pressure for 5 minutes.

bagara baingan
aubergine curry from hyderabad

serves: 4-6
soaking time: 10 minutes
preparation time: 30 minutes
cooking time: 40-45 minutes

500 gms small aubergines (baingan)
1½ tsp + 1 tsp salt or to taste
5-6 tbsp oil
1 tsp cumin seeds
½ tsp turmeric powder

ground to a smooth paste
2 medium-sized onions
1-2 cloves garlic (optional)
2 tbsp raw peanuts
2 tbsp grated dry coconut (copra)
1 medium lemon-sized ball of
tamarind, without seeds or strings
3-4 green chillies
1" piece ginger, grated
1 tbsp chopped coriander leaves
1 tsp coriander seeds
1 tsp cumin seeds
2 tbsp white sesame seeds (til),
roasted
¼ cup water

ground to a fine powder
2 x 1" sticks cinnamon
2-3 cloves
1 bay leaf
½ tsp black peppercorns
1 tsp poppy seeds (khus-khus),
powdered
½ tsp black cumin seeds (shah jeera)
1-2 black cardamoms

garnish
1 tbsp chopped coriander leaves

1. Cut aubergines in quarters, lengthwise and soak in water mixed with 1½ tsp salt for 10 minutes. Drain and set aside.

2. Heat 2 tbsp oil in a pan over moderate heat. Add aubergines and 1 tsp salt. Cook over low heat, tossing occasionally for about 10 minutes, till tender. Remove from heat and set aside.

3. Heat remaining oil in another pan over moderate heat. Sprinkle in cumin seeds and when they splutter, add turmeric powder and ground paste. Stir-fry for at least 20-25 minutes till spices are fragrant and oil floats to the surface.

4. Mix in spice powder and aubergines.

5. Pour in 1¼ cups water, mix gently and simmer for 5-6 minutes, stirring occasionally, till well blended.

6. Taste and add more salt if necessary.

7. Garnish with coriander leaves and serve hot with roti, paratha or puri.

note: The aubergines can also be cooked in the microwave oven. Coat thoroughly with 2 tsp oil, place in a microwave dish and cook on high for 5-6 minutes.

urulaikizhangu thayir pachadi
potato curd salad from tamil nadu

serves: 4-6
preparation time: 20 minutes
cooking time: 5 minutes

2 medium-sized potatoes
1½ cups fresh curd
1 tsp salt or to taste
½ tsp sugar

tempering
2 tsp oil
½ tsp mustard seeds
1 tsp cumin seeds
1 tsp husked black gram (urad dal)
1 tsp husked bengal gram (chana dal)
¼ tsp asafoetida powder (hing)
1 dried red chilli, halved
1 sprig curry leaves

garnish
1 tbsp finely chopped coriander leaves

1. Boil potatoes in their jackets. Peel and cut into ¼" cubes. Set aside.

2. Whisk curd with salt and sugar till well blended and smooth. Set aside.

3. Heat oil for tempering in a wok/frying pan. Add remaining ingredients for tempering in the order given. When mustard seeds splutter, add potatoes and sauté for 1-2 minutes. Remove from heat.

4. Set aside till cool. Gently stir in curd and garnish with coriander leaves.

5. Serve chilled or at room temperature.

pachaimilagai-kothamalli thayir pachadi
green chilli, coriander curd salad

serves: 4-6
preparation time: 10 minutes
cooking time: 5 minutes

1½ cups fresh curd
1 tsp salt or to taste

ground to a fine paste
2 green chillies
3 tbsp chopped coriander leaves
2 tbsp water

tempering
2 tsp ghee
½ tsp mustard seeds
1 tsp husked black gram (urad dal)
½ tsp asafoetida powder (hing)
1 dried red chilli, halved
1 sprig curry leaves

1. Whisk curd with salt till smooth. Blend in ground paste and set aside.

2. Heat ghee for tempering in a pan over moderate heat. Add remaining ingredients for tempering in the order given. When mustard seeds splutter, stir contents of pan into spiced curd.

3. Serve chilled or at room temperature as an accompaniment to any rice dish.

nellikai thayir pachadi
amla curd salad

serves: 4-6
preparation time: 10 minutes
cooking time: 5 minutes

1½ cups fresh curd
1 tsp salt or to taste

ground to a fine paste
¼ cup large variety of amla, seeded (see note alongside)
2-3 green chillies
2 tbsp grated fresh coconut
1-2 tbsp water

tempering
2 tsp oil
½ tsp mustard seeds
½ tsp asafoetida powder (hing)
1 dried red chilli, halved
1 tsp husked black gram (urad dal)
1 sprig curry leaves

garnish
1 tbsp finely chopped coriander leaves

1. Combine curd with salt and amla paste in a bowl. Whisk till well blended and smooth.

2. Heat oil for tempering in a frying pan over moderate heat. Add remaining ingredients for tempering in the order given. When mustard seeds splutter, stir contents of pan into pachadi.

3. Garnish with coriander leaves. Serve as a side dish.

note: The botanical name for amla is Emblica officinalis. It is a jade-green, tart fruit also known as the emblic gooseberry or Indian hog plum.

rice

masala sadam
spicy vegetable rice

serves: 4-6
preparation time: 20 minutes
cooking time: 20 minutes

1 cup basmati rice
2 tsp white butter
2 medium-sized carrots, finely chopped
1 medium-sized potato, finely chopped
¼ cup shelled green peas
2-3 tsp american sweet corn kernels
1 tsp salt or to taste
1½ tbsp lime juice

spice powder
2 tsp oil
2 tsp husked black gram (urad dal)
2 tsp husked bengal gram (chana dal)
2 dried red chillies
1 tbsp coriander seeds
½ tsp asafoetida powder (hing)
2-3 cloves
½" stick cinnamon
1 tbsp grated dry coconut (copra)

tempering
2 tbsp ghee
1 tsp mustard seeds
1 tsp husked black gram (urad dal)
½ tsp cumin seeds
1 dried red chilli, halved
1 sprig curry leaves

garnish
2 tbsp ghee
2 tbsp cashew nuts
2 tbsp finely chopped coriander leaves

1. Wash rice and drain. Add butter to rice and cook as given on page 12. Spread on a platter to cool.

2. Heat ghee for garnish in a pan over moderate heat and fry cashew nuts till golden. Remove from pan and set aside.

3. Heat oil for spice powder in the same pan. Add remaining ingredients for spice powder and fry over low heat. Toss gently, till dals turn golden and chillies and spices are fragrant. Cool and grind to a fine powder.

4. Heat ghee for tempering in a frying pan over moderate heat. Add remaining ingredients for tempering in the order given. When mustard seeds splutter, add vegetables and sauté for 1-2 minutes.

5. Pour in ½-¾ cup water, cover pan and simmer over low heat for 5-7 minutes, stirring occasionally, till vegetables are tender.

6. Add salt, spice powder and cooked rice. Stir gently till well blended.

7. Remove from heat. Sprinkle in lime juice and toss gently to mix.

8. Garnish with fried cashew nuts and coriander leaves and serve immediately or at room temperature.

note: This dish is a complete meal in itself when served with a thayir pachadi (pages 84, 85 or 86) and chips or fried appalams.

variation: Substitute green peas and sweet corn with a combination of sprouts. It will be nutritious and equally delicious.

kadugu tengai chitrannam
mustard coconut rice

serves: 4-6
preparation time: 20 minutes
cooking time: 15 minutes

1 cup basmati rice
1 tsp salt or to taste
2 tbsp lime juice

ground to a smooth paste
1 tbsp mustard seeds
3-4 dried red chillies
¾ cup grated fresh coconut
½ tsp turmeric powder
2-3 tbsp water

tempering
4 tbsp ghee
1 tsp mustard seeds
2 tsp husked black gram (urad dal)
½ tsp asafoetida powder (hing)
2 dried red chillies, halved
1 sprig curry leaves

1. Cook rice as given on page 12. Spread on a platter to cool.

2. Heat ghee for tempering in a frying pan over moderate heat. Add remaining ingredients for tempering in the order given. When mustard seeds splutter, blend in spice paste. Sauté for a minute and remove from heat.

3. Add rice, salt and lime juice to pan. Stir gently till well blended.

4. Serve immediately or at room temperature.

vendayakeerai sadam
fenugreek leaf rice

serves: 4-6
preparation time: 20 minutes
cooking time: 15 minutes

1 cup basmati rice
½ tsp turmeric powder
1 tsp salt or to taste
1-1½ cups tightly-packed fenugreek leaves (methi), finely chopped
2 tbsp lime juice

spice powder
2 tbsp ghee
2 tbsp husked black gram (urad dal)
1 tbsp coriander seeds
½ tsp cumin seeds
2-3 cloves
3-4 dried red chillies

tempering
4 tbsp ghee
½ tsp mustard seeds
1 tsp husked black gram (urad dal)
½ tsp asafoetida powder (hing)
1 dried red chilli, halved
1 sprig curry leaves

1. Cook rice as given on page 12. Spread on a platter to cool.

2. Heat ghee for spice powder in a wok/frying pan over moderate heat. Add remaining ingredients for spice powder and fry over low heat. Toss gently, till dal turn golden and spices and chillies are fragrant. Cool and grind to a fine powder.

3. Place fenugreek leaves in a pan over low heat and sprinkle in 1 tbsp water. Cover pan and cook for about 5 minutes, stirring occasionally, till tender. Remove from heat and set aside.

4. Heat ghee for tempering in a frying pan over moderate heat. Add remaining ingredients for tempering in the order given. When mustard seeds splutter, blend in fenugreek leaves and sauté for a minute.

5. Add spice powder and rice. Stir gently till well blended. Taste and add more salt if necessary.

6. Remove from heat and sprinkle in lime juice. Toss gently to mix.

7. Serve immediately or at room temperature.

note: If you are fond of the flavour of fenugreek leaves, increase the quantity, according to your taste. Some people do not like the bitter taste.

keerai sadam
amaranth leaf rice

serves: 4-6
preparation time: 20 minutes
cooking time: 15 minutes

1 cup basmati rice

2¼ cups tightly packed amaranth
leaves, finely chopped

1 tsp salt or to taste

2 tbsp lime juice

spice powder

2 tsp oil

3 tsp coriander seeds

1½ tsp cumin seeds

¾ tsp fenugreek seeds (methi)

½ tsp asafoetida powder (hing)

1 tsp black peppercorns

tempering

2 tsp oil or ghee

1 tsp mustard seeds

1 tsp husked black gram (urad dal)

1 tsp husked bengal gram
(chana dal)

1 dried red chilli, halved

1 sprig curry leaves

3 tbsp raw peanuts

1. Cook rice as given on page 12. Spread on a platter to cool.

2. Heat oil for spice powder in a frying pan over moderate heat. Add remaining ingredients for spice powder and fry over low heat. Toss gently, till spices are fragrant. Cool and grind to a fine powder.

3. Heat oil for tempering in the same pan over moderate heat. Add remaining ingredients for tempering in the order given. When mustard seeds splutter, add amaranth leaves and sauté for a minute.

4. Sprinkle in 2-3 tbsp water, cover pan partially and simmer over low heat for 3-4 minutes, stirring occasionally, till tender.

5. Add rice, spice powder and salt. Stir gently till well blended.

6. Remove from heat and sprinkle in lime juice. Toss gently to mix.

7. Serve hot or at room temperature.

alu gaddé bhath
potato rice from the
hebbar iyengar community of karnataka

serves: 4-6
preparation time: 20 minutes
cooking time: 20 minutes

1 cup basmati rice
500 gms baby potatoes
oil for deep frying
1 tbsp lime juice
1 tsp salt or to taste
1 sprig curry leaves

ground to a smooth paste
2 medium-sized onions
½ tsp black cumin seeds
(shah jeera)
2-3 cloves
1" stick cinnamon
1 tsp poppy seeds (khus-khus),
powdered
2 tbsp raw peanuts
½" piece ginger
2 green chillies
2 tbsp coriander leaves
1½ cups grated fresh coconut
¾ cup water

1. Cook rice as given on page 12. Spread on a platter to cool.

2. Boil potatoes in their jackets, cool and peel.

3. Heat oil for deep frying in a kadhai or deep frying pan over moderate heat. Fry potatoes in batches till golden. Drain and set aside.

4. Heat 1½ tbsp of the same oil in another frying pan over moderate heat. Add spice paste and fry over low heat for 5-7 minutes, till fragrant.

5. Add potatoes, lime juice and salt. Mix till potatoes are well coated with spices. Remove from heat.

6. Add rice and stir gently till well blended.

7. Heat ½ tbsp of the same oil in a small pan. Add curry leaves. When they splutter, pour contents of pan over rice. Toss gently to mix.

8. Serve hot or at room temperature.

Right : Pachamilagai-kothamalli thayir pachadi
(Green chilli, coriander curd salad) see page 85

kootaanchoru
vegetable, lentil and rice medley
from tirunelveli

serves: 4-6
soaking time: 10 minutes
preparation time: 40 minutes
cooking time: 30 minutes

1 cup basmati rice
¼ cup pigeon peas (tuvar/arhar dal)
1 medium lemon–sized ball of tamarind
2 drumsticks, cut into 3" pieces
½ cup finely chopped onion
¼ cup shallot, peeled and kept whole
½ cup finely chopped sheet beans
½ cup finely chopped french beans
¼ cup finely chopped carrot
½ cup finely chopped potato
½ cup finely chopped green plantain
½ cup finely chopped aubergine
1½ tsp salt or to taste
½ tsp turmeric powder

ground to a fine paste
1½ cups grated fresh coconut
10-12 dried red chillies
1 tsp cumin seeds
12-15 cloves garlic (optional)
1 cup water

tempering
3-4 tbsp oil
4 tbsp ghee
1 tsp mustard seeds
½ tsp asafoetida powder (hing)
½ tsp fenugreek seeds (methi)
1 sprig curry leaves

1. Cook rice as given on page 12. Cover and keep warm.

2. Wash dal and drain. Place dal in a pressure cooker with ½ cup water. Cook under pressure for 5 minutes.

3. Soak tamarind in 3 cups water for 10 minutes. Extract juice and discard pulp.

4. Heat 1½ cups water in a pan over high heat and boil drumsticks for 5-7 minutes. Set aside, reserving any remaining water.

5. Heat oil for tempering in a large pan Add remaining ingredients for tempering in the order given. When mustard seeds splutter, add onion and shallots. Sauté for 1-2 minutes.

6. Add remaining vegetables and sauté for 2 minutes.

7. Sprinkle in tamarind juice, salt and turmeric powder. Simmer for 18-20 minutes over low heat, stirring occasionally, till vegetables are tender.

8. Blend in cooked dal and ground paste.

9. Add rice, a few spoons at a time, mixing gently between each addition to blend well and prevent lumps.

10. Add drumsticks with its reserved water. If rice is too dry, sprinkle in a little more water. Stir gently and simmer for at least 5-7 minutes till well blended. Taste and add more salt if necessary

11. Serve hot.

note: Kootaanchoru is a complete meal by itself. You can serve it with roasted or fried appalam and a thayir pachadi (pages 84, 85 or 86) on the side.

Left : Beetroot parupu usili (Stir fried beetroot with lentil-crumble from Chettinad) see page 68

vendhaya thakkali sadam
fenugreek-flavoured tomato rice

serves: 4-6
preparation time: 20 minutes
cooking time: 10 minutes

1½ cups basmati rice

4-5 medium-sized tomatoes

2-3 green chillies, finely chopped

1" piece ginger, grated

3 medium-sized onions, finely chopped

½ tsp turmeric powder

1½ tsp salt or to taste

1 tbsp lime juice

¾ tsp fenugreek seeds (methi), roasted and powdered

tempering

3-4 tbsp oil

1 tsp mustard seeds

1 tsp husked black gram (urad dal)

1 tsp husked bengal gram (chana dal)

½ tsp asafoetida powder (hing)

1 dried red chilli, halved

1 sprig curry leaves

2 tbsp raw peanuts

garnish

2 tbsp finely chopped coriander leaves

1. Cook rice as given on page 12. Spread on a platter to cool.

2. Blanch tomatoes, peel and chop fine.

3. Heat oil for tempering in a frying pan over moderate heat. Add remaining ingredients for tempering in the order given. When mustard seeds splutter, add green chillies and ginger. Sauté for a minute.

4. Add onions and fry till golden.

5. Mix in tomatoes and turmeric powder. Sauté for 4-5 minutes till tomatoes are soft.

6. Add rice and salt. Lower heat and stir gently till well blended.

7. Remove from heat. Sprinkle in lime juice and powdered fenugreek. Toss gently to mix.

8. Garnish with coriander leaves and serve hot or at room temperature.

elumichampazham sadam
lime rice

serves: 4-6
preparation time: 25 minutes
cooking time: 10 minutes

1 cup basmati rice
2 tbsp raw peanuts
3-4 green chillies, finely chopped
½ tsp turmeric powder
1 tsp salt or to taste
2 tbsp lime juice

spice powder
2 tsp oil
1½ tsp husked bengal gram
(chana dal)
2 tsp coriander seeds
½ tsp fenugreek seeds (methi)
½ tsp asafoetida powder (hing)

tempering
2 tbsp oil
1 tsp mustard seeds
1 tsp husked black gram (urad dal)
1 tsp husked bengal gram
1 sprig curry leaves

1. Cook rice as given on page 12. Spread on a platter to cool.

2. Heat oil for spice powder in a frying pan over moderate heat. Add remaining ingredients for spice powder. Fry over low heat, tossing gently, till dal turns golden and spices are fragrant. Grind to a fine powder and set aside.

3. Heat oil for tempering in the same frying pan. Add remaining ingredients for tempering in the order given. When mustard seeds splutter, add peanuts and fry for 1-2 minutes.

4. Add green chillies, turmeric powder, salt, spice powder and rice. Stir gently till well blended.

5. Remove pan from heat and sprinkle in lime juice. Toss gently to mix.

6. Serve hot or at room temperature.

note: *A couple of onions, chopped and fried till golden can be added to lime rice as a variation.*

tengai sadam
coconut rice

serves: 4-6
preparation time: 25 minutes
cooking time: 10 minutes

1 cup basmati rice
1 tsp salt or to taste

spice powder
2 tsp + ¼ cup ghee
4-5 dried red chillies
1 tsp fenugreek seeds (methi)
½ tsp asafoetida powder (hing)
2 tbsp husked bengal gram (chana dal)
2 cups grated fresh coconut

garnish
2 tbsp + 2 tbsp ghee
2 tbsp cashew nut halves
2 tbsp raw peanuts

tempering
2 tsp ghee
1 tsp mustard seeds
1 tsp husked black gram (urad dal)
1 tsp husked bengal gram (chana dal)
1 dried red chilli, halved
2 green chillies, slit lengthwise
1 sprig curry leaves

1. Cook rice as given on page 12. Spread on a platter to cool.

2. Heat 2 tsp ghee for spice powder in a frying pan over moderate heat. Add red chillies, fenugreek seeds, asafoetida powder and dal. Fry over low heat, tossing gently, till chillies and spices are fragrant and till dal turns golden. Remove from pan and set aside.

3. Heat ¼ cup ghee in the same pan. Add coconut and fry over low heat, tossing gently till golden.

4. Combine all ingredients for spice powder and grind to a fine powder.

5. Heat 2 tbsp ghee for garnish in the same pan and fry cashew nuts till golden. Set aside.

6. Add 2 tbsp ghee to the same pan and fry peanuts till golden. Set aside.

7. Heat ghee for tempering in the same pan over moderate heat. Add remaining ingredients for tempering in the order given. When mustard seeds splutter, add rice, salt and spice powder.

8. Toss gently to mix and remove from heat.

9. Garnish with fried cashew nuts and peanuts.

10. Serve immediately or at room temperature.

pattani biryani
green pea biryani from kongunadu

serves: 4-6
soaking time: 30 minutes
preparation time: 15 minutes
cooking time: 35-40 minutes

2 cups basmati rice

6 tbsp oil

2 bay leaves

3-4 green cardamoms

1 " stick cinnamon

3-4 cloves

1 tsp fennel seeds (saunf)

¾ cup shallots, peeled and kept whole

2 tsp ginger-garlic paste

5-6 green chillies, slit lengthwise

3-4 tomatoes, finely chopped

½ cup chopped mint leaves

½ tsp turmeric powder

1½ tsp salt or to taste

1½ cups shelled green peas

2 tsp lime juice

garnish
¼ cup finely chopped coriander leaves

1. Wash rice and soak in water for 30 minutes. Drain and set aside

2. Heat oil in a heavy-based pan over moderate heat. Add bay leaves, cardamoms, cinnamon, cloves and fennel seeds. Sauté for a minute.

3. Add shallots and fry for about 5 minutes till golden.

4. Add ginger-garlic paste and green chillies. Cook for at least 5 minutes, stirring frequently.

5. Blend in tomatoes, and fry for 1-2 minutes.

6. Sprinkle in mint leaves, turmeric powder and salt. Fry for another minute.

7. Stir in green peas and 4 cups water and bring to boil over high heat.

8. Mix in rice and cook uncovered over low heat for 10-15 minutes till water is almost absorbed.

9. Cover pan tightly and place on a tawa over low heat. Cook for 8-10 minutes, till water is absorbed and rice is tender and fluffy.

10. Sprinkle in lime juice and coriander leaves. Toss gently to mix.

11. Serve hot.

zaffrani vegetable pulao
saffron vegetable rice from hyderabad

serves: 4-6
soaking time: 60 minutes
preparation time: 20 minutes
cooking time: 40 minutes

1½ cups basmati rice

2 bay leaves

2-3 green cardamoms

2 cloves

1" stick cinnamon

1 tsp + ½ tsp salt or to taste

1 tsp saffron strands

2 tbsp warm milk

3 tbsp + 2 tbsp + 1-2 tbsp ghee

4 onions, finely sliced

1 carrot, cut into ½" cubes

⅓ cup cauliflower florets

⅓ cup chopped (¼" pieces) french beans

1 potato, cut into ¼" cubes

½ cup shelled green peas

½-¾ cup fresh curd

1 tsp garam masala powder

1 tsp red chilli powder

ground to a paste

2-3 green chillies

1" piece ginger

½ tbsp water

garnish

2 tbsp chopped mint leaves

1. Wash rice and soak in 3 cups water for 1 hour. Drain well and set aside.

2. Place bay leaves, cardamoms, cloves, cinnamon, 1 tsp salt and 3 cups water in a pan over high heat and bring to boil.

3. Add rice and cook uncovered till water is almost absorbed. Cover pan tightly and place on a tawa or griddle over low heat. Cook till all the moisture is absorbed and rice is tender and fluffy.

4. Soak saffron in warm milk for 10 minutes.

5. Heat 3 tbsp ghee in a pan over moderate heat. Add onions and fry till golden. Remove from pan and set aside.

6. Heat 2 tbsp ghee in the same pan over moderate heat. Add remaining vegetables and ½ tsp salt. Stir-fry for 8-10 minutes, till tender. Remove from heat and set aside.

7. Heat remaining ghee in another pan over low heat. Add ground paste and fry for 1-2 minutes, till fragrant.

8. Blend in curd, garam masala powder and chilli powder and fry for about 5 minutes.

9. Add cooked vegetables and simmer for 1-2 minutes, stirring continuously, till well blended. (The vegetables should have very little moisture.)

10. Take a shallow pan and layer rice and vegetables twice, starting and ending with rice. Sprinkle with saffron milk, fried onions and mint leaves.

11. Cover pan tightly and place on a tawa or griddle over low heat for about 15-20 minutes.

12. Serve hot with mirchi ka salan (page **44**).

note: *The rice can also be cooked in a pressure cooker or microwave oven as given on page 12.*

nellikai sadam
amla rice

serves: 4-6
preparation time: 30 minutes
cooking time: 15 minutes

1 cup basmati rice
¼ cup + 1 cup (250 gms) grated
amla (see note alongside)
1 tsp salt or to taste

spice paste
¾ tsp mustard seeds
½ tsp asafoetida powder (hing)
6 dried red chillies
½ tsp turmeric powder
8 tbsp grated fresh coconut

tempering
3 tbsp oil
½ tsp mustard seeds
1 tbsp husked black gram (urad)
1 tbsp husked bengal gram (chana)
1 dried red chilli, halved
1 sprig curry leaves
⅓ cup raw peanuts

1. Cook rice as given on page12. Spread on a platter to cool.

2. Combine all ingredients for spice paste with ¼ cup amla and ¼ cup water. Grind to a smooth consistency.

3. Heat oil for tempering in a heavy-based pan over moderate heat. Add remaining ingredients for tempering in the order given. When mustard seeds splutter, dals turn golden and peanuts are fried, add 1 cup amla.

4. Stir-fry over low heat for 4-5 minutes, till amla is tender.

5. Blend in spice paste and fry for another 3-4 minutes, stirring frequently, till spices are fragrant.

6. Add salt and rice. Toss gently till well blended.

7. Serve hot with a thayir pachadi (pages 84, 85 or 86), fried appalams or potato wafers.

note: The botanical name for amla is Emblica officinalis. It is a jade-green, tart fruit also known as the emblic gooseberry or Indian hog plum.

godumai pulliyogaray
tangy wheat lapsi from north arcot

serves: 4-6
soaking time: 10 minutes
preparation time: 15 minutes
cooking time: 20-25 minutes

1½ cups broken wheat (lapsi)
1 large lime-sized ball of tamarind
1 tbsp ghee
2 tbsp cashew nuts, halved
2 tsp salt or to taste

spice powder
1 tsp husked black gram (urad dal)
1 tsp husked green gram
(mung dal)
6 dried red chillies
1 tsp white sesame seeds (til)
1½ tsp fenugreek seeds (methi)
½ tsp asafoetida powder (hing)
½ tsp black peppercorns
1 sprig curry leaves

tempering
½ cup oil
1 tsp mustard seeds
½ tbsp husked bengal gram
(chana dal)
½ cup shelled peanuts
1 sprig curry leaves

1. Wash broken wheat well and drain. Place broken wheat in a pressure cooker container with 3 cups water. (Add sufficient water to the cooker body.) Cook under pressure for 5 minutes. Spread on a platter to cool.

2. Soak tamarind in 1½ cups water for 10 minutes. Extract juice and discard pulp.

3. Heat ghee in a pan over moderate heat. Fry cashew nuts till golden. Drain and set aside.

4. Combine all ingredients for spice paste and roast in a dry frying pan over low heat. Toss gently, till dals turn golden and chillies and spices are fragrant. Cool and grind to a fine powder.

5. Heat oil for tempering in a pan over moderate heat. Add remaining ingredients for tempering in the order given. When mustard seeds splutter, add tamarind juice, salt and spice powder.

6. Simmer till water has evaporated and mixture has a jam-like consistency. Remove from heat.

7. Place wheat in a large bowl and gradually blend in tamarind jam. Mix well. Taste and add more salt if required.

8. Garnish with fried cashew nuts and serve at room temperature.

snacks

dosai
rice pancakes

makes: 13-14 dosai
soaking time: 6 hours
preparation time: 40 minutes
fermentation time: 8-10 hours
cooking time: 1 hour

1½ cups regular rice

*1 cup parboiled rice
(ukda/sela chaval)*

*½ cup husked black gram
(urad dal)*

1½ tsp fenugreek seeds (methi)

2 tsp salt or to taste

oil for shallow frying

1. Combine regular and parboiled rice, wash well and soak in water for 6 hours.

2. Combine dal and fenugreek seeds, wash well and soak in water for 6 hours.

3. Drain rice and grind to make a smooth batter, gradually adding 1-1¾ cups water.

4. Drain dal and grind till light and fluffy, gradually adding ½-¾ cup water.

5. Combine both batters in a large container, mix in salt and set aside to ferment for 8-10 hours. (Use a fairly tall container, since the fermented batter will become a mass of bubbles and increase in volume.)

6. Add a little water if necessary to make a thick batter of pouring consistency.

to prepare tawa
7. Heat a tawa or griddle over high heat till it sizzles when a few drops of water are sprinkled on it.

8. Lower heat and smear a very thin film of oil evenly over tawa. (Do not use too much oil, as batter will not spread evenly.)

to cook dosai
9. Pour a ladle of batter into centre of tawa. Spread quickly using a circular motion with back of ladle to form a 6" round dosai.

10. Drizzle 1 tsp oil around edges. Raise heat and cook for 1-2 minutes till base is golden brown.

11. Turn over carefully and fry the other side till crisp and golden and remove from heat.

12. Sprinkle water on tawa after making each dosai so that it doesn't get overheated, and oil it again.

13. If a dosai appears to be getting burnt, wipe the tawa with a wet cloth. Remove all burnt pieces and continue.

14. Serve hot with vengaya sambar (page 19), tengai chutney (page 152) or vengaya gojju (page 162).

note: *Use a halved potato/aubergine/onion dipped in oil to spread oil evenly over tawa.*

The leftover batter can be stored in the refrigerator for a couple of days.

It is best to keep a separate tawa for dosai. Don't use the tawa on which you make roti. After cleaning it, smear with a little oil and store. A non-stick tawa, of course, is excellent for a novice. It's so easy to use.

variations: *Add 1 cup of chopped amaranth leaves to the batter. Mix well and make* **mollakerai dosai (amaranth leaf pancake).**

Sprinkle 1 tbsp grated fresh coconut on the dosai while frying the first side to make **tengai dosai (coconut pancake).**

vendayakeerai dosai
fenugreek leaf pancake

makes: 8-10 dosai
soaking time: 2 hours
preparation time: 20 minutes
cooking time: 30 minutes

½ cup regular rice
I cup husked green gram
(mung dal)
½ cup grated fresh coconut
4-5 dried red chillies
I small marble-sized ball of
tamarind, without seeds or strings
¾ cup tightly packed fenugreek
leaves (methi), finely chopped
I ½ tsp salt or to taste
oil for shallow frying

1. Combine rice and dal, wash well and drain. Soak in 3 cups water for 2 hours.

2. Drain and mix in coconut, red chillies and tamarind.

3. Grind to make a smooth batter, gradually adding 1-1¼ cups water. Add a little extra water if necessary to make a batter of thick pouring consistency.

4. Mix in fenugreek leaves and salt.

5. Prepare tawa and cook dosai as given on page 104.

6. Serve hot with tengai chutney (page 152).

godumai dosai
wheat pancake

makes: 14-16 dosai
soaking time: 6 hours
preparation time: 40 minutes
fermentation time: 6 hours
cooking time: 45 minutes

I ½ cups wheat grains (gehun)
½ cup husked black gram
(urad dal)
I tsp fenugreek seeds (methi)
I ½ tsp salt or to taste
oil for shallow frying

1. Wash wheat grains and soak in water for 6 hours.

2. Combine dal and fenugreek seeds. Wash and soak in water for 6 hours.

3. Drain wheat grains and grind to make a smooth batter, gradually adding 1-1½ cups water.

4. Drain dal and grind till light and fluffy, gradually adding about ½-1 cup water.

5. Combine both batters, mix in salt and set aside to ferment for 6 hours. Add a little water if necessary, to make a batter of thick pouring consistency.

6. Prepare tawa and cook dosai as given on page 104.

7. Serve hot with tengai chutney (page 152).

thavalai dosai

rice and black gram pancake
from north arcot

makes: 17-18 dosai
soaking time: 30 minutes
preparation time: 30 minutes
cooking time: 30 minutes

You will need an appachatti (described on page 10) to make this dish.

1 cup regular rice

½ cup husked black gram (urad dal)

1 cup sour curd

2-3 dried red chillies, ground to a paste

1 tsp salt or to taste

½ tsp asafoetida powder (hing)

oil for shallow frying

1. Wash rice and soak in 2 cups water for 30 minutes.

2. Wash dal and soak in water for 30 minutes.

3. Drain rice and grind to make a fine batter, gradually adding ½-¾ cup water.

4. Drain dal and grind to make a fine batter, gradually adding ¼-½ cup water.

5. Combine both batters. Blend in sour curd, chilli paste, salt and asafoetida powder.

6. Set aside for about 15-20 minutes.

7. Place a deep frying pan or appachatti over moderate heat. Dip a piece of cloth in oil and smear pan evenly with oil.

8. Pour a small ladle of batter into centre of pan. Hold pan with both handles and quickly swirl it around so that batter coats base and sides of pan evenly and spreads to form a 6" round dosai.

9. Cover pan and cook over low heat for 5-7 minutes till base and edges are golden and centre is spongy. When done, the dosai will come away from the sides.

10. Gently remove dosai with a spatula and serve hot with dosai milagai podi (page 160) or any chutney of choice.

11. Sprinkle water on appachatti after making each dosai so that it doesn't get over-heated, and oil it again.

note: *Increase the quantity of ground chillies to make it spicier.*

maida dosai
refined flour pancake

makes: 8-9 dosai
preparation time: 15 minutes
fermentation time: 2 hours
cooking time: 30 minutes

½ cup refined flour (maida)

½ cup rice flour

½ cup sour curd

1 tsp salt or to taste

1 medium-sized onion, finely chopped

oil for shallow frying

ground to a paste

½ cup grated fresh coconut

3-4 green chillies

2 tbsp chopped coriander leaves

1 tbsp water

tempering

2 tsp ghee

½ tsp mustard seeds

½ tsp cumin seeds

¼ tsp asafoetida powder (hing)

1 sprig curry leaves

1. Combine both the flours in a large container. Add curd and mix till well blended.

2. Add ½ cup water, a little at a time, whisking all the while to make a smooth, thick batter of pouring consistency.

3. Mix in salt and set aside to ferment for 2 hours.

4. Blend onion and coconut paste into batter.

5. Heat ghee for tempering in a frying pan over moderate heat. Add remaining ingredients for tempering in the order given. When mustard seeds splutter, stir contents of pan into batter.

6. Prepare tawa and cook dosai as given on page 104. (Pour in a large ladle of batter to make a ¼" thick dosai.)

7. Serve hot with vengaya gojju (page 162) or any chutney of choice.

note: This is a quick, tasty dosai, which does not require pre-planning, hence a great snack for hungry children and unexpected guests.

minapapindi dosai
quick pancake from andhra pradesh

makes: 7-8 dosai
preparation time: 10 minutes
cooking time: 20 minutes

1½ cups dosai flour (see note alongside)

1 tsp salt or to taste

1 large onion, finely chopped

2 green chillies, finely chopped

2 tbsp chopped coriander leaves

oil for shallow frying

1. Place dosai flour in a mixing bowl with salt. Gradually add 1½-2 cups water and mix to make a smooth, thick batter of pouring consistency.

2. Add onion, green chillies and coriander leaves. Mix well.

3. Prepare tawa and cook dosai as given on pages 104.

4. Serve hot with cobri pachadi (page 156).

note: To make dosai flour, combine 4 parts regular rice and 1 part husked black gram (urad dal) and get it milled into a fine flour. Excess flour can be stored in an airtight container and used as required.

atukula dosai
parched rice pancake from andhra pradesh

makes: 12-14 dosai
soaking time: 2 hours
fermentation time: 4 hours
preparation time: 45 minutes
cooking time: 45 minutes

2 cups regular rice

1 cup parched rice (poha)

1 tbsp husked black gram (urad dal)

2 cups sour curd whisked with 2 cups water

¼ tsp sodium bicarbonate

1 tsp salt or to taste

oil for shallow frying

1. Wash rice, parched rice and dal. Drain and soak in diluted curd for 2 hours. Drain and reserve soaking liquid.

2. Grind to a smooth batter, gradually adding 1½-2 cups soaking liquid.

3. Mix in sodium bicarbonate and salt. Set aside to ferment for 3-4 hours.

4. Prepare tawa and cook dosai as given on page 104. (Take a large ladle of batter to form a ¼" thick dosai.) After drizzling oil around the edges, cover tawa and cook for 1-2 minutes till base is crisp and golden and top is soft and spongy. Remove from heat. (It is cooked on one side only.)

5. Serve hot with cobri pachadi (page 156).

challaatlu
sour curd pancake from andhra pradesh

makes: 8-9 dosai
fermentation time: 8-10 hours
preparation time: 20 minutes
cooking time: 30 minutes

1 cup rice flour

2 cups sour curd

¼ tsp sodium bicarbonate

1 tsp salt or to taste

1 tbsp husked green gram
(mung dal)

2 medium-sized onions, finely
chopped

4 green chillies, finely chopped

1" piece ginger, grated

2 tbsp finely chopped coriander
leaves

oil for shallow frying

1. Combine rice flour, sour curd, sodium bicarbonate
   and salt in a large container. Mix well and set aside
   to ferment for 8-10 hours.

2. Soak dal in ¼ cup water for 30 minutes before
   making dosai. Drain well and add to rice flour batter.

3. Mix in onions, green chillies, ginger and
   coriander leaves.

4. Prepare tawa and cook dosai as given on page104.

5. Serve hot with allam pachadi (page 155) or vengaya
   chutney (page 154).

note: This is a simple uncomplicated recipe – very useful for
a busy person, who doesn't have the time to go through the
tedious task of grinding the dosai batter.

Right :Tengai sadam
(Coconut rice) see page 96

vendaya oothappam
fenugreek and rice pancake

makes: 6-7 oothappam
soaking time: 2 hours
fermentation time: 8-10 hours
preparation time: 40 minutes
cooking time: 40 minutes

½ *cup regular rice*

½ *cup parboiled rice
(ukdal/sela chaval)*

*2 tbsp husked black gram
(urad dal)*

1 tbsp pigeon peas (tuvar/arhar)

1 tsp fenugreek seeds (methi)

1 tsp salt or to taste

oil for shallow frying

1. Combine all ingredients except salt and oil in a large container. Add 2 cups water and set aside to soak for 2 hours.

2. Drain and grind to make a coarse batter, gradually adding ¾-1¼ cups water.

3. Mix in salt and set aside to ferment for 8-10 hours.

4. Add a little water if necessary to make a thick batter of pouring consistency.

5. Prepare tawa and cook oothappam as given for dosai on pages 104. (Take a large ladle of batter to form a ¼" thick oothappam.)

6. Serve hot with dosai milagai podi (page 160) and tengai chutney (page 152).

Left : Alu gaddé bhath (Potato rice from the Hebbar Iyengar community of Karnataka) see page 92

masala oothappam
spicy pancakes

makes: 12-14 oothappam
soaking time: 6 hours
preparation time: 10 minutes
fermentation time: 10-12 hours
cooking time: 30 minutes

*1½ cups parboiled rice
(ukda/sela chaval)*
*½ cup husked black gram
(urad dal)*
1 tsp fenugreek seeds (methi)
1½ tsp salt or to taste
ghee or oil for shallow frying

topping
*8-10 tsp dosai milagai podi
(page 160)*
1 cup chopped coriander leaves

1. Wash rice and soak in water for 6 hours. Combine dal with fenugreek seeds, wash and soak in water for 6 hours.

2. Drain rice and grind to make a smooth batter, gradually adding 1-1¼ cups water.

3. Drain dal and grind till light and fluffy, gradually adding ½-¾ cup water.

4. Combine both batters, mix in salt and set aside to ferment and get a little sour for 10-12 hours.

5. Add a little water if necessary, to make a batter of thick pouring consistency.

6. Prepare tawa as given for dosai on page 104.

7. Pour a large ladle of batter into centre of tawa to make ¼" thick oothappam. Do not spread the batter thin like a dosai. Drizzle 1 tsp ghee or oil around edges. Sprinkle 1 tsp dosai milagai podi evenly over oothappam. Cover with 2 tbsp of coriander leaves.

8. Raise heat and cook for 1-2 minutes till base is golden brown. Turn over carefully and fry the other side till crisp and golden.

9. Serve hot with vengaya sambar (page 19) and tengai chutney (page 152).

javvarisi oothappam
rice and sago pancakes

makes: 10-12 oothappam
soaking time: 1 hour
preparation time: 1½ hours
cooking time: 1 hour

1 cup sago (sabudana)

1 cup regular rice

2 tbsp sour curd

2 onions, finely chopped

2 tbsp finely chopped coriander leaves

1½ tsp salt or to taste

oil for shallow frying

ground to a paste

4-6 green chillies

½" piece ginger, grated

1 tbsp water

1. Wash sago and soak in water for 1 hour. Wash rice and soak in water for 1 hour.

2. Drain rice and grind to a coarse batter, gradually adding ¾-1 cup water.

3. When rice is half-ground add sago and grind till smooth, gradually adding ¾-1 cup water.

4. Mix in sour curd, onions, coriander leaves, salt and ground paste.

5. Add more water if necessary to make a batter of thick, dropping consistency.

6. Prepare tawa and cook oothappam as given for dosai on pages 104. (Take a large ladle of batter to form a ¼" thick oothappam and cook on both sides.)

7. Serve hot with dosai milagai podi (page 160) or tengai chutney (page 152).

muzhu ulundu adai
black gram pancake

makes: 7-8 adai
soaking time: 1 hour
preparation time: 10 minutes
cooking time: 30 minutes

*1 cup parboiled rice
(ukda/sela chaval)*

*¼ cup whole black gram
(sabut urad)*

5-6 dried red chillies

½ tsp asafoetida powder (hing)

1 sprig curry leaves

*2 tbsp finely chopped coriander
leaves*

2 tbsp sour curd

1½ cups grated fresh coconut

1¼ tsp salt or to taste

oil for shallow frying

1. Wash rice and soak in water for 1 hour. Wash dal and soak in water for 1 hour.

2. Drain rice and grind to make a coarse batter, gradually adding 1-1½ cups water.

3. Drain dal and grind to make a fine batter, adding red chillies, asafoetida powder and 1 tbsp water.

4. Combine both batters. Mix in curry leaves, coriander leaves, sour curd, coconut and salt. Add more water if necessary to make a thick batter of pouring consistency.

5. Prepare tawa as given for dosai on page 104.

6. Pour a large ladle of batter into centre of tawa. Spread it out quickly using a circular motion with back of ladle to form a 6" round adai. Make a ¼" hole in the centre with a spatula. Cook till base is golden.

7. Turn carefully and fry the other side till crisp and golden.

8. Serve hot with dosai milagai podi (page 160) and tengai chutney (page 152).

ragi adai
finger millet pancakes

makes: 10-12 adai
preparation time: 15 minutes
cooking time: 30 minutes

2 cups ragi flour (finger millet)

¼ cup whole wheat flour (atta)

¼ cup rice flour

2 medium-sized onions, finely chopped

½ cup grated fresh coconut

4 green chillies, finely chopped

1" piece ginger, grated

2 tbsp finely chopped coriander leaves

1 sprig curry leaves

1½ tsp salt or to taste

a piece of banana leaf

oil for shallow frying

1. Combine all ingredients, except banana leaf and oil, in a bowl.

2. Gradually sprinkle in ¾-1 cup water and knead well to form a soft, pliable dough.

3. Pass banana leaf over a flame to wilt it. Oil it lightly.

4. Heat a tawa over moderate heat.

5. Place banana leaf on the counter. Oil your hands and pinch off a large lime-sized ball of dough. Pat dough with your fingers to form a 5" round adai on the leaf.

6. Gently lift the leaf and flip it on to the hot tawa. The leaf will stick to the adai. When the adai starts to cook, the leaf will come off easily. Gently peel it off.

7. Drizzle oil around and over adai and cook on both sides till done.

8. Use the same piece of banana leaf to make remaining adai, oiling the leaf and your hands as required.

9. Serve with tengai chutney (page 152).

note: Ragi is also called hill millet.

pesharattu
mung pancake from andhra pradesh

makes: 11-12 pesharattu
soaking time: 2 hours
preparation time: 15 minutes
cooking time: 30 minutes

2 cups whole mung (sabut mung)

¼ cup rice

1 tsp salt or to taste

2 tbsp chopped coriander leaves

2-3 cloves garlic (optional)

½" piece ginger, grated

3 medium-sized onions, finely chopped

5-6 green chillies, finely chopped

oil for shallow frying

1. Wash mung and rice and drain. Soak in water for 2 hours.

2. Drain and mix in salt, coriander leaves, garlic (if used) and ginger. Grind coarsely, gradually adding 1¾-2¼ cups water.

3. Prepare tawa as given for dosai on page 104.

4. Pour a ladle of batter into centre of tawa. Spread it out quickly using a circular motion with back of ladle to form a 6" round dosai.

5. Drizzle 1 tsp oil around edges. Sprinkle a tbsp of chopped onions and ½ tsp of green chillies. Cook till base is golden. Turn carefully and fry the other side till crisp and golden.

6. Serve hot with allam pachadi (page 155).

variation: **pesharu pindi pakoda (mung fritters):**
Leftover pesharattu batter can be used to make delicious fritters. Add 1 sprig curry leaves to the batter. Heat plenty of oil in a deep frying pan over high heat. Drop spoonfuls of batter into hot oil. Lower heat to moderate and fry pakoda in batches turning frequently till brown and crisp. Drain and place on kitchen paper to absorb excess oil.

arisi idli
steamed rice cakes
You will need an idli rack (described on page 10) to prepare this dish.

makes: 14-15 idli
soaking time: 6 hours
fermentation time: 8 hours
preparation time: 10 minutes
cooking time: 20 minutes

½ cup regular rice

½ cup parboiled rice (ukda/sela chaval)

½ cup husked black gram (urad dal)

½ tsp fenugreek seeds (methi)

1½ tsp salt or to taste

oil for brushing idli rack

1. Combine regular rice and parboiled rice. Wash well and soak in water for 6 hours.

2. Combine dal and fenugreek seeds. Wash and soak in water for 6 hours.

3. Drain rice and grind to make a coarse batter, gradually adding ½-1 cup water.

4. Drain dal and grind to make a smooth frothy batter, gradually adding ¼-¾ cup water.

5. Combine both batters, mix in salt and set aside to ferment for 8 hours. The batter should have a thick pouring consistency. Add more water if necessary.

to steam idli

6. Brush an idli rack with oil. Spoon ¼ cup batter into each depression. Place rack in a pressure cooker, close cooker and steam for 15-20 minutes (without the weight). Insert a toothpick into idli to check if cooked; it should come out clean.

7. Allow rack to cool for 1-2 minutes and ease out idli with the help of a knife.

8. Serve hot with vengaya sambar (page 19), tengai chutney (page 152) and milagai podi (page 160).

aval idli
steamed parched rice cakes
You will need an idli rack (described on page 10) to prepare this dish.

makes: 17-18 idli
soaking time: 2 hours
fermentation time: 8 hours
preparation time: 2 hours
cooking time: 30 minutes

1½ cups regular rice

*¼ cup husked black gram
(urad dal)*

½ tsp fenugreek seeds (methi)

*½ cup parched rice (poha),
washed and drained*

1½ tsp salt or to taste

1 tbsp sour curd

1¼ cups grated fresh coconut

4 green chillies, finely chopped

½ tsp grated ginger

2 tbsp chopped coriander leaves

oil for brushing idli rack

tempering
3 tbsp ghee
1 tsp mustard seeds
1 tsp cumin seeds
½ tsp asafoetida powder (hing)
1 sprig curry leaves

1. Wash rice and soak in water for 2 hours. Combine dal and fenugreek seeds. Wash and soak in water for 1 hour.

2. Drain rice and grind to make a coarse batter, gradually adding ¾-1 cup water.

3. Drain dal, add parched rice and grind to make a smooth batter, gradually adding ½-¾ cup water.

4. Combine both batters and mix in salt and sour curd. Set aside to ferment for 8 hours.

5. Just before making idli, heat ghee for tempering in a small pan over moderate heat. Add remaining ingredients for tempering in the order given. When mustard seeds splutter, pour contents of pan into batter.

6. Mix in coconut, green chillies, ginger and coriander leaves. The batter should be thicker than dosai batter, but have a pouring consistency. Add more water if necessary.

7. Steam idli as given on page117.

8. Serve hot with vengaya sambar (page 19) and tengai chutney (page 152).

masala idli
spicy steamed cake from north arcot
You will need an idli rack (described on page 10) to prepare this dish.

makes: 6-7 idli
soaking time: 30 minutes
fermentation time: 4 hours
preparation time: 20 minutes
cooking time: 20 minutes

1 dried red chilli

½ cup husked green gram (mung dal)

3 tbsp grated fresh coconut

3 green chillies

1 marble-sized ball of tamarind, without seeds or strings

½" piece ginger, grated

1 sprig curry leaves

1 tsp salt or to taste

oil for brushing idli rack

1. Roast red chilli in a pan till it changes colour and is fragrant. Set aside.

2. Wash dal and soak in 1 cup water for 30 minutes. Drain dal and combine with roasted red chilli, coconut, green chillies, tamarind and ginger.

3. Grind to make a coarse batter, gradually adding 1-1½ cups water.

4. Mix in salt and curry leaves.

5. Set aside to ferment for 4 hours.

6. The batter should have a thick pouring consistency. Add more water if necessary.

7. Steam idli as given on page 117.

8. Serve hot with vengaya sambar (page 19) and tengai chutney (page 152).

kanchipuram idli
spicy steamed rice cakes from north arcot
You will need an idli rack (described on page 10) to prepare this dish.

makes: 20-22 idli
soaking time: 8 hours
fermentation time: 8-10 hours
preparation time: 40 minutes
cooking time: 40 minutes

*1 cup parboiled rice
(ukda/sela chaval)*

*1 cup husked black gram
(urad dal)*

½ tsp black peppercorns

¼ tsp ginger powder (saunth)

1 tsp salt or to taste

2 tbsp oil

2 tbsp ghee

½ tsp asafoetida powder (hing)

1 sprig curry leaves

oil for brushing idli rack

1. Wash rice and soak in water for 8 hours. Wash dal and soak in water for 8 hours.

2. Drain rice and grind to a coarse batter, gradually adding ½-¾ cup water.

3. Drain dal, add peppercorns and ginger powder and grind to make a coarse batter, gradually adding 1-1½ cups water.

4. Combine both batters, mix in salt and set aside to ferment for 8-10 hours.

5. The batter should be thicker than dosai batter, but have a pouring consistency. Add more water if necessary.

6. Just before making idli, heat oil and ghee in a small pan. Add asafoetida powder and curry leaves. When curry leaves splutter, mix contents of pan into batter.

7. Steam idli as given on page 117.

8. Serve hot with vengaya sambar (page 19) and tengai chutney (page 152).

semiya idli
steamed vermicelli cakes
You will need an idli rack (described on page 10) to prepare this dish.

makes: 15-16 idli
soaking time: 1 hour
preparation time: 15 minutes
cooking time: 15 minutes

*2 tbsp husked bengal gram
(chana dal – optional)*

*1¼ tbsp + 1½ tbsp + 1 tbsp +
1 tbsp oil + extra for brushing
idli rack*

*1½ cups fine vermicelli (sevian),
broken into 1" pieces*

1 cup fine semolina (sooji/rava)

2 tbsp broken cashew nuts

*1 medium-sized onion, finely
chopped*

2¼ cups sour curd

3-4 green chillies, finely chopped

1 sprig curry leaves

1 tbsp chopped coriander leaves

1" piece ginger, grated

1 tsp salt or to taste

1. Soak dal (if used) in ½ cup water for 1 hour.
   Drain and set aside.

2. Heat 1¼ tbsp oil in a frying pan over moderate heat.
   Add vermicelli and fry till golden, tossing gently.
   Transfer to a bowl and set aside.

3. Pour 1½ tbsp oil into the same pan, heat through
   and fry semolina, stirring continuously, till it turns
   pink. Add to bowl containing vermicelli.

4. Pour 1 tbsp oil into the same pan, heat through and
   fry cashew nuts till golden. Add to bowl.

5. Heat 1 tbsp oil in the same pan over moderate heat
   and fry onions till golden. Transfer to bowl.

6. Add soaked dal (if used), sour curd, green chillies,
   curry leaves, coriander leaves, ginger and salt
   to bowl.

7. Mix well. It should be a thick batter.

8. Steam idli as given on page 117.

9. Serve hot with vengaya sambar (page 19) and
   tengai chutney (page 152).

heeraykai bajji
ridge gourd fritters from karnataka

makes 25-30 bajjis
preparation time: 20 minutes
cooking time: 30 minutes

2 medium-sized ridge gourds
(toori)
oil for deep frying

batter
1 cup gram flour (besan)
2 tbsp rice flour
1 tsp salt or to taste

ground to a fine powder
½ tsp mustard seeds
½ tsp black peppercorns
1½ tsp coriander seeds
1 tsp cumin seeds
½ tsp red chilli powder
½ tsp asafoetida powder (hing)
½ tsp tamarind powder or
½ marble-sized ball of tamarind,
without seeds and strings

1. Peel ridge gourd and cut into fine slices.

2. Combine ingredients for batter and mix in spice powder.

3. Gradually sprinkle in ½-¾ cup water and mix to make a smooth, thick batter of pouring consistency. Add 1-2 tbsp water if necessary to achieve the right consistency.

4. Heat oil in a deep frying pan to smoking point. Dip ridge gourd slices in batter and slide gently into oil. Lower heat to moderate and fry in batches turning frequently, till golden brown and crisp.

5. Drain and place on kitchen paper to absorb excess oil.

6. Serve hot with tengai chutney (page 152).

thulasi vadai
wild basil patties from kongunadu

makes: 16-18 vadai
soaking time: 1 hour
preparation time: 15 minutes
cooking time: 30 minutes

¾ cup husked bengal gram (chana dal)

3 dried red chillies

1 tsp fennel seeds (saunf)

1 tsp cumin seeds

2 medium-sized onions, finely chopped

1 tsp salt or to taste

¼ cup chopped wild basil (thulasi/tulsi)

oil for deep frying

1. Wash dal and soak in water with red chillies, fennel seeds and cumin seeds for 1 hour.

2. Drain and grind to make a coarse batter, gradually adding ⅓-½ cup water.

3. Add onions, salt and basil. Mix well.

to shape and fry vadai

4. Heat oil in a deep frying pan to smoking point.

5. Wet your hands, take a ladle of batter and flatten it into a 2" round patty. Slip gently into hot oil.

6. Fry vadai in batches over moderate heat, turning frequently, till golden brown and crisp.

7. Drain and place on kitchen paper to absorb excess oil.

8. Serve hot with any chutney of choice.

note: Thulasi/tulsi is also called holy basil or ram basil.

variation: You can substitute the basil with mint leaves. It will taste equally delicious.

mundiriparuppu vadai
cashew nut patties

makes: 16-18 vadai
soaking time: 30 minutes
preparation time: 15 minutes
cooking time: 30 minutes

¾ cup husked bengal gram
(chana dal)
3-4 green chillies, finely chopped
1 dried red chilli
½" piece ginger, grated
½ tsp asafoetida powder (hing)
1 tsp salt or to taste
3 tbsp rice flour
2 medium-sized onions, finely
chopped
2 tbsp finely chopped coriander
leaves
¾ cup cashew nuts, chopped
oil for deep frying

1. Wash dal and soak in 2 cups water for 30 minutes.

2. Drain dal and grind to a thick, coarse batter with green chillies, red chilli, ginger and asafoetida powder, gradually adding 5-6 tbsp water.

3. Just before frying the vadai, mix in salt, rice flour, onions, coriander leaves and cashew nuts.

4. Shape and fry vadai as given on page 123.

5. Serve hot with tengai chutney (page 152).

note: The batter can be made a day ahead and stored in the refrigerator. Add salt just before frying, else it could turn sour.

thavalai adai
cocktail patties from tamil nadu

makes: 35-37 adai
soaking time: 2 hours
preparation time: 30 minutes
cooking time: 1 hour

¼ cup husked bengal gram
(chana dal)

¼ cup pigeon peas (tuvar/arhar)

3 green chillies

1-2 dried red chillies

½ tsp asafoetida powder (hing)

1 cup coarsely broken rice
(rice rava)

¾ cup grated fresh coconut

1¼ tsp salt or to taste

2 tbsp chopped coriander leaves

1 sprig curry leaves

oil for shallow frying

tempering

1 tbsp sesame oil (til ka tael)

½ tsp mustard seeds

½ tsp cumin seeds

½ tsp husked black gram
(urad dal)

½ tsp husked bengal gram
(chana dal)

1 sprig curry leaves

1. Combine both dals and wash. Drain and soak in
   2 cups water for 2 hours.

2. Drain dals and grind to a thick, coarse batter with
   green chillies, red chillies and asafoetida powder,
   gradually adding ¼ cup water.

3. Heat oil for tempering in a deep frying pan. Add
   remaining ingredients for tempering in the order
   given. When mustard seeds splutter, add 4 cups
   water and bring to boil over high heat.

4. Lower heat and stir in batter, broken rice, coconut
   and salt. Simmer for 18-20 minutes, stirring
   continuously, till water is completely absorbed and
   ingredients are well cooked.

5. Blend in coriander leaves and curry leaves.
   Remove from heat and cool.

6. When cool enough to handle, knead well and shape
   into 2" round adai.

7. Heat a deep frying pan over moderate heat. Place a
   few adai in the centre of pan. Drizzle 2 tsp oil
   around adai. Cover pan and cook for 5-7 minutes
   over low heat. The base should be crisp and brown,
   while the top will be soft. Remove from pan
   and drain.

8. Prepare remaining adai in the same manner.

9. Serve hot with any chutney of choice.

note: Rice rava is readily available in some cities. If
unavailable, have the rice milled coarsely to resemble rava.
Sift it, discard flour and use contents in the sieve.

variations: The adai can be shallow fried on a tawa.

Both sides can be fried till crisp and golden.

muttacose bonda
cabbage balls

makes: 22-23 bonda
soaking time: 1 hour
preparation time: 20 minutes
cooking time: 30 minutes

*¼ cup husked bengal gram
(chana dal)*

¼ cup pigeon peas (tuvar/arhar)

2 tbsp rice grains

3-4 dried red chillies

1 green chilli

4 tbsp finely shredded cabbage

*2 tbsp finely chopped coriander
leaves*

1 tsp salt or to taste

oil for deep frying

1. Combine both dals with rice. Wash and soak together in 1½ cups water for 1 hour.

2. Drain dals and rice and grind to a coarse dough with red chillies and green chilli, gradually adding 5-6 tbsp water.

3. Mix in cabbage, coriander leaves and salt.

4. Heat oil in a deep frying pan to smoking point. Shape dough into small lime-sized balls, lower heat to moderate and deep fry bonda in batches, till golden.

5. Drain and place on kitchen paper to absorb excess oil.

6. Serve hot with tengai chutney (page 152).

*Right : Masala oothappam
(Spicy pancakes) see page 112*

vendayakeerai bonda
fenugreek leaf balls

makes: 12-13 bonda
soaking time: 1 hour
preparation time: 15 minutes
cooking time: 30 minutes

½ cup husked green gram
(mung dal)
2 tbsp gram flour (besan)
1-2 tbsp rice flour
1 onion, finely chopped
4 green chillies, finely chopped
1 tbsp chopped fenugreek leaves
(methi)
1 tsp salt or to taste
oil for deep frying

1. Wash dal and soak in 1 cup water for 1 hour. Drain and grind to make a smooth dough, gradually adding 2-3 tbsp water.

2. Stir gram flour, rice flour, onion, green chillies, fenugreek leaves and salt into dough.

3. Mix well. Add up to 1 tbsp water if necessary. It should be a firm dough.

4. Heat oil in a deep frying pan to smoking point.

5. Shape dough into small lime-sized balls. Slip 6-8 bonda into hot oil. Lower heat to moderate and fry bonda in batches, turning frequently, till golden brown and crisp.

6. Drain and place on kitchen paper to absorb excess oil.

7. Serve hot with tengai chutney (page 152).

note: *Do not add too much water while making the dough. You will not be able to shape the bonda. In case it is not firm enough to shape, add extra rice flour to thicken it.*

Left : Urulaikizhangu somasi
(Spicy potato-filled pastry) see page 128

urulaikizhangu somasi
spicy potato-filled pastry

makes: 14-15 samosi
preparation time: 30 minutes
cooking time: 30 minutes

filling
4-5 medium-sized potatoes
8-10 cashew nuts, finely chopped
¾ tsp salt or to taste
*1 tbsp finely chopped coriander
leaves*

ground to a smooth paste
4 dried red chillies
½ tsp cinnamon powder
½ tsp cumin seeds
¼ tsp fennel seeds (saunf)
1-2 tsp water

dough
1½ cups refined flour (maida)
½ tsp salt or to taste
1 tsp butter
oil for deep frying

1. Boil potatoes in their jackets. Peel and mash well.

2. Add cashew nuts, salt, coriander leaves and spice paste to potatoes. Mix till well blended and set aside.

3. Sift flour and salt into a bowl. Rub in butter till it resembles breadcrumbs. Add ⅓-½ cup water gradually, and knead to make a stiff dough. Knead for at least 10 minutes till smooth and pliable.

4. Divide dough into 14-15 equal portions.

5. On a floured board, roll each portion of dough into a 4" disc. Place a tbsp of filling along one half a disc.

6. Dab a little water along the edges, and fold the other half over filling to cover completely and form a semicircle. Flatten gently and seal the edges by pressing down with a fork. Make remaining somasi in the same way.

7. Heat oil in a deep frying pan till smoking. Lower heat to moderate and fry somasi in batches, turning frequently, till golden and crisp.

8. Drain and place on kitchen paper to absorb excess oil.

9. Serve hot with any chutney of choice.

note: This is the South Indian version of the North Indian samosa.

gundu pongla
rice and lentil dumplings from karnataka
You will need a paniyaramchatti (described on page 10) to make this dish.

makes: 65-70 gundu pongla
soaking time: 4 hours
preparation time: 30 minutes
fermentation time: 8 hours
cooking time: 1½ hours

2 cups regular rice

¼ cup parboiled rice
(ukda/sela chaval)

½ cup husked bengal gram
(chana dal)

½ cup husked black gram
(urad dal)

¼ cup husked green gram
(mung dal)

¼ cup parched rice (poha)

1½ tsp salt or to taste

1" piece ginger, grated

2 tbsp finely chopped coriander
leaves

oil for deep frying

tempering

2 tbsp oil

1 tsp mustard seeds

2 medium-sized onions, finely
chopped

6 tbsp grated fresh coconut

1. Combine regular and parboiled rice, wash and soak in water for 4 hours.

2. Combine all dals, wash and soak in water for 4 hours.

3. Drain rice and grind to make a fine batter, gradually adding 1-1½ cups water.

4. Add parched rice and grind once more to a smooth consistency.

5. Drain dals and grind to make a fine batter, gradually adding ½ cup water.

6. Combine both batters, mix in salt and set aside to ferment for 8 hours.

7. Add more water if necessary to make a batter of thick pouring consistency.

8. Heat oil for tempering in a frying pan over moderate heat. Add mustard seeds. When they splutter, add onions and fry for 1-2 minutes. Mix in coconut and stir-fry for a minute.

9. Stir contents of pan into batter.

10. Mix in ginger and coriander leaves.

11. Heat a paniyaramchatti and fill a quarter of each depression with oil. When heated, add batter to come halfway up the depressions. Fry over low heat for 2-3 minutes.

12. Turn gundu pongla over gently with a skewer and fry the other side for 2-3 minutes, till golden. Drain and place on kitchen paper to absorb excess oil.

13. Prepare remaining gundu pongla in the same way. Serve hot with any chutney of choice.

moru appam
savoury rice dumplings

You will need a paniyaram chatti (described on page 10) to make this dish.

makes: 48-50 appam
preparation time: 20 minutes
cooking time: 30 minutes

*3 cups leftover dosai batter
(page 104)*
*½ cup sour curd (optional – see
note alongside)*
1" piece ginger, grated
3-4 green chillies, finely chopped
2 tbsp chopped coriander leaves
*¼ cup cubed (¼" cubes) fresh
coconut*
1 tsp salt or to taste
oil for deep frying

tempering
1 tsp oil
1 tsp mustard seeds
1 tsp husked black gram (urad dal)
½ tsp asafoetida powder (hing)
1 sprig curry leaves

1. Combine dosai batter with sour curd (if used), ginger, green chillies, coriander leaves, coconut and salt. Mix well.

2. Heat oil for tempering in a small pan over moderate heat. Add remaining ingredients for tempering in the order given. When mustard seeds splutter, stir contents of pan into batter and mix well.

3. Heat a paniyaramchatti and fill quarter of each depression with oil. When heated, add batter to come halfway up the depressions. Fry over low heat for 2-3 minutes.

4. Turn appam over gently with a skewer and fry the other side for 2-3 minutes till golden.

5. Drain and place on kitchen paper to absorb excess oil.

6. Prepare remaining appam in the same way.

7. Serve hot with dosai milagai podi (page 160) or any chutney of choice.

note: If the leftover batter is old and already sour, sour curd is not required.

pathiri
rice bread from kerala

makes: 10 pathiri
preparation time: 5 minutes
cooking time: 30 minutes

½ tsp salt or to taste

½ tsp oil

1 cup fine rice flour + extra for rolling

1. Add salt and oil to 1½ cups water in a pan and bring to boil over high heat.

2. Lower heat and add rice flour whisking continuously to avoid lumps. Cook for 7-8 minutes, till all the water is absorbed.

3. Remove from heat and set aside till cool enough to handle.

4. Knead well without adding more water to make a soft, pliable dough.

5. Divide dough into 10 small balls. Sprinkle with rice flour and roll out into thin 5" round discs. Trim edges with a cutter.

6. Heat a tawa or griddle over moderate heat. Place a pathiri on tawa and cook both sides till it puffs up like a phulka.

7. Remove from heat and serve with vegetable stew. It makes a hearty breakfast tiffin.

note: Use a whisk while adding rice flour to the water. This will prevent lumps.

puli aval
tamarind-flavoured parched rice

serves: 4-6
soaking time: 10 minutes
preparation time: 15 minutes
cooking time: 15 minutes

2 cups parched rice (poha)

1 medium lemon-sized ball of tamarind

1 tsp salt or to taste

½ tsp sambar powder (page 14)

½ tsp turmeric powder

4 green chillies, finely chopped

tempering

3-4 tbsp sesame oil (til ka tael)

1 tsp mustard seeds

1 tsp cumin seeds

1 tsp husked black gram (urad dal)

1 tsp husked bengal gram (chana dal)

½ tsp asafoetida powder (hing)

1 dried red chilli, halved

1 sprig curry leaves

garnish

2 tbsp chopped coriander leaves

1. Wash parched rice and drain.

2. Soak tamarind in 1½ cups water for 10 minutes. Extract juice and discard pulp.

3. Add salt, sambar powder and turmeric powder to tamarind juice. Mix well and set aside for 10-15 minutes.

4. Heat oil for tempering in a frying pan over moderate heat. Add remaining ingredients for tempering in the order given. When mustard seeds splutter, add green chillies and sauté for about 2 minutes.

5. Stir in tamarind juice. Simmer for 10-15 minutes till the raw aroma of tamarind disappears.

6. Sprinkle in parched rice. Simmer uncovered, stirring occasionally, till all moisture is absorbed and rice is dry. This will take 2-3 minutes.

7. Garnish with coriander leaves.

8. Serve hot with fried papad or potato wafers. It makes a good light meal.

note: There are different varieties of parched rice available in the market. The red one, which is hand-pounded, is more nutritious. If using this variety, soak the rice for 10 minutes after washing it and drain.

godumai pongal
wheat kedgeree

serves: 4-6
preparation time: 5 minutes
cooking time: 20 minutes

2 tbsp + 3 tbsp ghee
1 cup broken wheat (daliya)
*½ cup husked green gram
(mung dal)*
½ tsp turmeric powder
1½ tsp salt or to taste
½ cup grated fresh coconut
1 sprig curry leaves

coarsely ground
1 tsp cumin seeds
1 tsp black peppercorns

1. Heat 2 tbsp ghee in a frying pan over moderate heat. Add broken wheat and fry over low heat for at least 5 minutes, stirring continuously.

2. Add dal and fry for 1-2 minutes.

3. Sprinkle in turmeric powder and salt. Give it a stir and transfer to a pressure cooker.

4. Pour in 4 cups water. Cook under pressure for 5-7 minutes. Allow pressure to fall on its own before opening cooker.

5. Transfer pongal to a frying pan. Add remaining ghee, coconut, curry leaves and spice powder.

6. Mix well and remove from heat.

7. Serve hot with milagai karimeedu (page 161) and any chutney of choice.

variation: Use wheat lapsi in place of daliya.

molla keerai pongal
amaranth leaf kedgeree

serves: 4-6
preparation time: 15 minutes
cooking time: 20 minutes

½ cup husked green gram
(mung dal)

1 cup rice

1 tsp salt or to taste

½ tsp turmeric powder

1 cup finely chopped amaranth
leaves

4 tbsp + 2 tbsp ghee

2 medium-sized onions, finely
chopped

coarsely ground

2-3 cloves

½" stick cinnamon

2-3 green cardamoms

¾ tsp black peppercorns

1. Wash dal and rice and drain. Place in a pressure
   cooker with salt, turmeric powder and
   4½ cups water. Cook under pressure for 5 minutes.

2. Place amaranth leaves in a frying pan with ¼ cup
   water and simmer over low heat for 5 minutes,
   till tender.

3. Combine cooked dal and rice and amaranth leaves in
   a pan over low heat with 4 tbsp ghee, spice powder
   and ½ cup water. Taste and add salt if required.
   Simmer, stirring gently, till well blended. Add more
   water if required, the texture should be that of
   a moist khichdi.

4. Heat 2 tbsp ghee in another pan and fry onions over
   moderate heat till golden. Add to pongal.

5. Mix well and serve hot with vengaya gojju (page162).

masala kadalaika
crunchy fried peanuts

makes: 500 gms
preparation time: 15 minutes
cooking time: 30 minutes

1 cup gram flour (besan)
¼ cup rice flour
2 tsp red chilli powder
1 tsp asafoetida powder (hing)
1½ tsp salt or to taste
1 tbsp ghee
2½ cups raw peanuts with skin
oil for deep frying

1. Combine gram flour, rice flour, chilli powder, asafoetida powder and salt in a bowl. Stir in ⅓ - ½ cup water. Mix well to form a spreadable batter.

2. Melt ghee in a pan and blend into batter.

3. Smear batter evenly over peanuts.

4. Heat oil in a deep frying pan till smoking. Drop peanuts into hot oil and fry in batches over moderate heat, till golden brown. Drain and place on kitchen paper to absorb excess oil.

5. The crunchy peanuts can be cooled and stored in an airtight jar and served whenever required.

6. It is a great cocktail or teatime snack.

variation: Halved cashew nuts can be substituted for peanuts. It will taste equally delicious.

thukda
fried savoury biscuits

makes: 400-450 gms
preparation time: 15 minutes
cooking time: 30 minutes

2 cups refined flour (maida) +
extra for rolling
1 tsp salt or to taste
¼ tsp sodium bicarbonate
½ cup melted ghee
2 tsp curd
oil for deep frying

1. Sift flour with salt and sodium bicarbonate into a bowl. Mix in ghee and curd.

2. Gradually add ¼-½ cup water and knead to make a stiff dough. Set aside for 10 minutes.

3. Divide dough into 9-10 equal portions.

4. On a floured surface, roll each portion into a 6" disc. With a sharp knife cut each disc into ½" wide wedges.

5. Heat oil in a deep frying pan till smoking. Slip thukda into hot oil. Lower heat to moderate and fry thukda in batches, turning frequently, till golden brown and crisp.

6. Drain and place on kitchen paper to absorb excess oil.

7. When cool, store in an airtight container. Serve as a snack with tea.

variation: **Inippu thukda (fried sweet biscuits):** *Place fried thukda into a thick sugar syrup made by boiling 1 cup sugar with ½ cup water for 7-8 minutes. Spread out on a large platter to cool and dry; the thukda will be coated with sugar.*

omappodi
crispy noodles from tamil nadu

makes: about 400 gms
preparation time: 15 minutes
cooking time: 30 minutes

You will need a thenkuzhal press (described on page 10) to make this dish.

1 cup roasted bengal gram (bhuna chana), powdered

2 cups gram flour (besan)

¼ cup rice flour

1 tsp ajwain, coarsely crushed

1-1½ tsp red chilli powder

1 tsp asafoetida powder (hing)

2 tbsp ghee or unsalted butter

1½ tsp salt or to taste

oil for deep frying

1. Combine roasted gram flour, gram flour, rice flour, ajwain, chilli powder, asafoetida powder, ghee or butter and salt in a mixing bowl.

2. Mix well with your fingers until it resembles breadcrumbs.

3. Gradually add ¾-1 cup water and knead to make a stiff dough.

4. Heat oil in a pan till smoking. Add 2 tbsp hot oil to dough and knead well.

5. Use a thenkuzhal press to make the omappodi. Fill its container with dough and press dough out in noodles. Move the press in circles as you press out the dough, so that omappodi falls into the oil in a circular shape.

6. Fry till the hissing sound ceases and it is golden and crisp.

7. Remove with a slotted spoon and place on kitchen paper to absorb excess oil.

8. Cool and store in airtight jars. They stay crisp for a couple of weeks.

note: Omappodi is the South Indian version of the North Indian sev.

ribbon pakoda
ribbon crisps from tamil nadu

makes: about 500 gms
preparation time: 20 minutes
cooking time: 30 minutes

You will need a thenkuzhal press (described on page 10) to make this dish.

1 cup rice flour

2 cups gram flour (besan)

2-3 tsp red chilli powder

1 tsp asafoetida powder (hing)

2 tbsp unsalted butter

1½ tsp salt or to taste

1 tsp white sesame seeds (til)

oil for deep frying

1. Combine all ingredients except oil for frying in a bowl. Mix thoroughly with your fingers till butter is well incorporated and it resembles breadcrumbs. Gradually add ¾-1 cup water and knead to make a firm dough.

2. Heat oil in a deep frying pan till smoking.

3. Add 1 tbsp hot oil to dough and knead again. Insert the ribbon pakoda disc (with two ½" slits running along its diameter) in a thenkuzhal press. Fill container with dough and press dough out in ribbons into hot oil. With a slotted spoon break ribbons into convenient lengths to facilitate even cooking.

4. Turn ribbons and fry till the hissing sound ceases and they are golden and crisp.

5. Remove with a slotted spoon and place on kitchen paper to absorb excess oil.

6. Cool and store in airtight jars. They remain crisp for a couple of weeks.

note: Since the ribbons can resemble a tape, it is also called tape pakoda.

variation: Instead of adding red chilli powder to the dough, add 2 tsp ground green chillies. You will get lighter coloured ribbon pakoda.

Right top : Fill container with dough
Right bottom : Press dough out in ribbons into hot oil

godumai uppuma
vegetable and wheat pilaf

serves: 4-6
preparation time: 20 minutes
cooking time: 25 minutes

tempering

2 tbsp oil or ghee

1 tsp mustard seeds

1 tsp husked black gram (urad dal)

½ tsp asafoetida powder (hing)

1 dried red chilli, halved

1 sprig curry leaves

uppuma

2 medium-sized onions, finely chopped

3-4 green chillies, finely chopped

½" piece ginger, grated

1 cup chopped mixed vegetables – potatoes, carrots, french beans – and green peas and cauliflower florets

1 tsp salt or to taste

½ tsp turmeric powder

1 cup broken wheat (daliya)

1 tbsp lime juice

garnish

2 tbsp chopped coriander leaves

1. Heat oil or ghee for tempering in a heavy frying pan over moderate heat. Add remaining ingredients for tempering in the order given. When mustard seeds splutter, add onions, green chillies and ginger. Sauté for 1-2 minutes.

2. Add all vegetables, salt, turmeric powder and 3 cups water. Bring to boil. Lower heat and simmer for 5-7 minutes, till vegetables are tender.

3. Gradually add broken wheat, 2-3 tbsp at a time, stirring continuously to prevent lumps.

4. Cook uncovered over low heat for 12-15 minutes till broken wheat is tender and water is completely absorbed. Add more water and cook for a few minutes longer if daliya is not tender.

5. Remove from heat. Sprinkle in lime juice and mix well.

6. Garnish with chopped coriander leaves and serve hot.

note: Uppuma wheat (daliya) is available in most South Indian stores. If unavailable, buy good quality wheat, clean it and have it milled coarsely to resemble semolina. Sift, discard the powdered flour and use the contents inside the sieve.

Left : Ribbon pakoda
(Ribbon crisps from Tamil Nadu) see page 138

uppuma kozhakattay
steamed rice dumplings
You will need an idli rack (described on page 10) to prepare this dish.

makes: 15-17 dumplings
preparation time: 10 minutes
cooking time: 35 minutes

tempering

2 tbsp coconut oil

1 tsp mustard seeds

1 tsp husked black gram (urad dal)

1 dried red chilli, halved

½ tsp asafoetida powder (hing)

1 sprig curry leaves

dumplings

1½ tsp salt or to taste

2 tbsp grated fresh coconut

2 cups broken rice and pigeon pea mix (see note alongside)

oil for brushing idli rack

1. Heat oil for tempering in a pan over moderate heat. Add remaining ingredients for tempering in the order given. When mustard seeds splutter, pour in 7 cups water and bring to boil. Add salt and coconut.

2. Lower heat and add broken rice and pigeon pea mix and cook for 15-18 minutes, stirring frequently, till water is completely absorbed.

3. Remove from heat and set aside till uppuma is completely cool.

4. Shape uppuma into 2" oval dumplings. Arrange dumplings in a greased idli stand and place in a pressure cooker. Steam for 10-15 minutes (without the weight). You can also use a regular steamer. Serve hot with tengai thuvaiyal (page 164).

note: To make broken rice and pigeon pea mix, combine 5 cups (1 kg) rice, ½ cup (100 gms) pigeon peas (tuvar/arhar) and 1½ tsp black peppercorns. Grind coarsely in a mixer grinder. Sift and discard flour. Use contents inside the sieve. Measure out 2 cups of broken rice and pigeon pea mix from the sieve to make uppuma kozhakattay. Store remaining mix in an airtight container.

sweets

tengai kadalaimavu burfi
coconut gram flour sweets

makes: 40-45 burfi
preparation time: 10 minutes
cooking time: 40 minutes

1 tbsp + ¼ cup + ¾ cup ghee
1 cup gram flour (besan)
1 cup grated fresh coconut
1 cup milk
3 cups sugar

1. Grease a thali or flat steel plate which has a 1" rim with 1 tbsp ghee and set aside.

2. Heat ¼ cup ghee in a frying pan over low heat. Add gram flour and fry for about 2 minutes, stirring continuously till the raw aroma disappears.

3. Transfer gram flour to a heavy-based pan and add ¾ cup ghee, coconut, milk and sugar. Simmer on low heat, stirring continuously till mixture is thick and starts to leave sides of pan.

4. Pour mixture on to greased thali. Gently smoothen surface of burfi with a spatula.

5. While still hot, cut into the desired shapes.

6. Remove from plate when cool.

7. Serve with tea or coffee.

8. It can be stored in an airtight container for 3-4 days.

tengai burfi
coconut sweets

makes: 28-30 burfi
preparation time: 15 minutes
cooking time: 45 minutes

2 tsp ghee

4 cups milk

3 cups sugar

2 cups grated fresh coconut

1. Grease a steel thali or flat plate that has a 1" rim with ghee and set aside.

2. Combine milk, sugar and coconut in a heavy-based pan over moderate heat. Cook, stirring continuously, for 40-45 minutes, till mixture is thick and starts to leave sides of pan.

3. Pour mixture on to greased thali. Gently smoothen surface of burfi with a spatula and allow to cool.

4. Cut into small squares or diamond shaped pieces and serve.

note: This sweet is quaintly referred to as '432' according to the proportions of the ingredients used in the recipe.

badam tengai burfi
almond and coconut sweets

makes: 25-28 burfi
soaking time: 2 hours
preparation time: 20 minutes
cooking time: 35-40 minutes

1 cup + 2 tbsp almonds
1¼ cups grated fresh coconut
2 tbsp poppy seeds, powdered
1 cup milk
1 tbsp + 1 cup ghee
1¼ cups sugar
1 tsp vanilla or cardamom essence

1. Soak all almonds in 2 cups hot water for 2 hours. Peel almonds.

2. Chop 2 tbsp almonds into thin slivers for garnish and set aside.

3. Grind remaining almonds with coconut and poppy seeds to a smooth paste, gradually adding milk.

4. Grease a steel thali or flat plate that has a 1" rim with 1 tbsp ghee and set aside.

5. Place ground paste, sugar and ½ cup water in a heavy-based pan over low heat,

6. Add 1 cup ghee and simmer, stirring continuously to prevent burning. Keep stirring till mixture starts leaving sides of pan. (This will take 35-40 minutes.)

7. Stir in essence, remove from heat and pour on to greased thali. Gently smoothen surface of burfi with a spatula.

8. Garnish with almond slivers.

9. When cool, cut into desired shape and size.

10. Store in an airtight container for up to 2-3 days.

variation: Instead of making burfi, you can also roll it into small marble-sized balls.

payatha laadu
green gram sweets

makes: 12-15 laadu
preparation time: 10 minutes
cooking time: 10 minutes

*1 cup husked green gram
(mung dal)*
1 cup powdered sugar
5-6 green cardamoms, powdered
½ cup ghee
¼ cup cashew nuts, chopped

1. Roast dal in a dry frying pan over low heat for 3-4 minutes, stirring frequently, till golden.

2. Remove from heat and grind to a fine powder with sugar and cardamom powder.

3. Heat 1 tbsp ghee in a frying pan over low heat. Add cashew nuts and fry till golden. Add to dal mixture.

4. Heat remaining ghee in the same pan and add to laadu mixture. Mix till well incorporated and shape into small lime-sized balls.

note: Make sure the dal is powdered really fine. Sift the ground mixture to be sure; otherwise the laadu will break easily.

kadalaimavu laadu
gram flour sweets

makes: 12-15 laadu
preparation time: 10 minutes
cooking time: 10 minutes

¾ cup ghee
1 cup gram flour (besan)
½ cup milk
¾ cup powdered sugar
*6 almonds, blanched and cut into
¼" pieces*
*6 seedless raisins (kishmish),
chopped*
6 green cardamoms, powdered

1. Heat ghee in a frying pan over low heat. Add gram flour and cook for 3-4 minutes, stirring continuously, till the raw aroma disappears and it turns golden.

2. Remove from heat and add milk, stirring vigorously to avoid lumps. Set aside to cool a little.

3. Mix in sugar, almonds, raisins and cardamom powder.

4. Shape into small lime-sized balls. These laadus break easily. Handle carefully while storing in an airtight container.

payatham parupu payasam
green gram dessert

serves: 4-6
preparation time: 30 minutes
cooking time: 20 minutes

¾ cup husked green gram (mung dal)

3 cups grated fresh coconut

1½ cups powdered jaggery

¼ cup sugar or to taste

2 tbsp ghee

garnish

2 tbsp + 1 tbsp + 1 tbsp ghee

2 tbsp cashew nuts, halved

2 tbsp seedless raisins (kishmish)

¼ cup cubed (¼" cubes) fresh coconut

½ tsp powdered green cardamom

1. Wash dal and drain.
2. Place dal in a pressure cooker with 1½ cups water. Cook under pressure for 3 minutes. Whisk dal and set aside.
3. Mix grated coconut with 2 cups hot water. Process for 1-2 minutes in a blender. Pour liquid through a strainer lined with muslin cloth and press out thick coconut milk.
4. Add ¾ cup hot water to coconut residue. Blend and strain once more to get the second extract. Repeat to get the third extract. Set aside.
5. Heat 2 tbsp ghee for garnish and fry cashew nuts till golden. Set aside.
6. Add 1 tbsp ghee to the same pan and fry raisins till they puff up. Set aside.
7. Add 1 tbsp ghee and fry coconut cubes till golden. Set aside.
8. Combine jaggery and ½ cup water in a heavy-based pan. Simmer till jaggery melts and dissolves. Strain through a muslin cloth to remove dirt.
9. Return jaggery syrup to pan and add cooked dal, and 2 tbsp ghee. Simmer for 5-6 minutes till well blended.
10. Pour in third extract of coconut milk and simmer for about 2 minutes.
11. Add second extract of coconut milk and simmer for 3-4 minutes.
12. Taste payasam and add sugar as required.
13. Stir till sugar melts and add thick coconut milk. Heat through, stirring continuously and remove from heat. Do not allow it to curdle.
14. Add fried cashew nuts, raisins and coconut. Sprinkle cardamom powder and mix well.
15. Serve hot or at room temperature.

ghasgase payasam
poppy seed dessert from karnataka

This is a delicious dessert made by the hebbar iyengar community of karnataka.

serves: 4-6
soaking time: 30 minutes
preparation time: 10 minutes
cooking time: 15 minutes

¼ cup almonds, blanched and peeled

⅓ cup poppy seeds, powdered

2 tbsp rice grains

½ cup grated fresh coconut

2 tbsp grated dry coconut (copra)

1½ cups powdered jaggery

4-5 green cardamoms, powdered

1. Grind almonds to a smooth paste adding 3-4 tbsp water.

2. Combine poppy seeds and rice. Soak in water for 30 minutes. Drain and grind to a fine paste, gradually adding ¼ cup water.

3. Combine fresh and dry coconut. Add 3-4 tbsp water and grind to a smooth paste.

4. Dissolve jaggery in 2 cups water in a heavy-based pan over moderate heat. Strain through a fine muslin cloth to remove dirt.

5. Return jaggery syrup to pan and place over low heat. When hot, add almond paste, poppy seed paste and coconut paste, stirring continuously to avoid lumps.

6. Add ½-1 cup water if payasam is too thick. It should be of pouring consistency. Remove from heat and add powdered cardamoms.

7. Serve hot or chilled.

aval payasam
parched rice dessert

serves: 4-6
soaking time: 1 hour
preparation time: 10 minutes
cooking time: 1 hour

1 cup parched rice (poha)

9¼ cups (2 litres) full cream milk

¾-1 cup sugar

1 tsp saffron strands soaked in 2 tbsp milk

1. Soak rice in water for 1 hour. Drain and set aside.

2. Place milk in a heavy-based pan over moderate heat and simmer for 45-50 minutes till reduced to about 1½ litres.

3. Mix in rice and simmer for 10-12 minutes, stirring frequently, till tender. Remove from heat.

4. Add sugar and keep stirring till dissolved.

5. Mix in saffron with its soaking liquid.

6. Serve hot or chilled.

paravaannam
rice dessert from andhra pradesh

serves: 4-6
soaking time: 30 minutes
preparation time: 10 minutes
cooking time: 45-50 minutes

½ cup rice

7-8 cups full cream milk

2 tbsp sago (sabudana)

1½ cups powdered jaggery

3 tbsp ghee

3 tbsp cashew nuts, halved

2 tbsp seedless raisins (kishmish)

½ tsp powdered green cardamom

1. Wash rice and drain. Soak rice in water for 30 minutes. Drain and set aside.

2. Place milk in a heavy-based pan over high heat and bring to boil. Lower heat and simmer for 10-15 minutes till reduced by about one-third.

3. Add sago and simmer for 10 minutes

4. Mix in rice and simmer for at least 15-20 minutes till tender.

5. In another pan combine jaggery and ¼ cup water. Cook and stir till jaggery dissolves. Strain jaggery through a muslin cloth into payasam.

6. Meanwhile, heat 1½ tbsp ghee in a frying pan over moderate heat and fry cashew nuts till golden. Drain and set aside.

7. Add remaining ghee to pan and fry raisins till they puff up. Drain and set aside.

8. Add cashew nuts, raisins and powdered cardamoms to payasam. Simmer for 5 minutes.

9. Serve hot or chilled.

double ka meetha
bread pudding from hyderabad

serves: 5-6
preparation time: 1 hour
cooking time: 30 minutes

2 tsp ghee + extra for deep frying

3¾ cups (750 ml) milk

1 cup sugar

*1 tsp saffron strands soaked in
1 tbsp warm milk*

*6 slices bread, cut into quarters
(crusts discarded)*

½ cup khoya, crumbled

½ cup almonds, thinly slivered

½ cup pistachios, finely chopped

½ tsp powdered green cardamom

1 cup whipped cream (optional)

1. Grease a shallow serving dish with 2 tsp ghee. Set aside.

2. Place milk in a heavy-based pan over high heat and bring to boil. Lower heat and keep stirring, till milk thickens. It should reduce to about 500 ml. Cool and set aside.

3. Combine sugar and 1 cup water in a pan and bring to boil. Remove scum. Boil till it reaches a syrup of one string consistency. (Dip your index finger into a teaspoon of syrup. Touch the syrup on the finger with your thumb and move it back. The syrup should form a string.)

4. Mix in saffron with its soaking liquid and remove from heat.

5. Heat ghee for deep frying in a frying pan. Fry bread in batches till crisp and golden. Drain and set aside.

6. Dip fried bread in sugar syrup and arrange half the slices in the greased dish. Sprinkle half the khoya over bread. Pour half the thickened milk on top. Sprinkle with half the almonds, pistachio and powdered cardamom.

7. Repeat layering.

8. Pour remaining sugar syrup around the bread.

9. Preheat oven to 100°C and place dish in oven. Bake for 10-15 minutes. This will help in allowing the layers to set.

10. Alternately place the dish on a griddle over low heat for 10-15 minutes taking care not to burn the base.

11. Serve hot or chilled topped with whipped cream.

note: If you find thickening the milk tedious, use evaporated milk. Condensed milk is not recommended since it will make it too sweet and cloying.

ethekka appam
sweet plantain fritters from kerala

makes: 16-18 appam
preparation time: 10 minutes
cooking time: 30 minutes

6 ripe plantains
1 cup refined flour (maida)
½ cup rice flour
1 tsp sugar
a pinch of sodium bicarbonate
oil for deep frying

1. Peel plantains and slice lengthwise into 3 pieces. Combine flour, rice flour, sugar and sodium bicarbonate in a bowl. Gradually add 1½-2 cups water and mix to make a smooth thick batter of pouring consistency. Add more water if necessary.

2. Heat oil in a deep frying pan to smoking point. Dip plantains in batter and slip gently into hot oil.

3. Lower heat to moderate and fry plantains in batches, turning frequently till golden brown and crisp.

4. Drain and place on kitchen paper to absorb excess oil.

note: *Traditionally these fritters are made with nendrampazham – a special variety of plantains available only in Kerala. You can use any variety of plantain.*

accompaniments

tengai chutney
coconut chutney

makes: 1-1¼ cups
preparation time: 10 minutes
cooking time: 5 minutes

1 cup grated fresh coconut
¼ cup roasted bengal gram
(bhuna chana)
3-4 green chillies
½" piece ginger, grated
2 tbsp chopped coriander leaves
¾ tsp salt or to taste
¾ cup sour curd

tempering
1 tsp oil
½ tsp mustard seeds
½ tsp cumin seeds
1 tsp husked black gram (urad dal)
½ tsp asafoetida powder (hing)
1 dried red chilli, halved
1 sprig curry leaves

1. Combine coconut, gram, green chillies, ginger, coriander leaves and salt. Grind to a smooth consistency, gradually adding ¼-⅓ cup water.

2. Add sour curd and mix well.

3. Heat oil for tempering in a frying pan over moderate heat. Add remaining ingredients for tempering in the order given. When mustard seeds splutter, stir contents of pan into tengai chutney. Mix well.

4. Serve with any dosai, idli, vadai, pakoda or adai of choice.

note: If you prefer a thicker chutney, grind the ingredients with curd, and don't add any water.

pudina chutney
mint chutney

makes: 1 cup
preparation time: 20 minutes
cooking time: 5 minutes

2 tsp oil

3–4 green chillies

*1 tbsp husked black gram
(urad dal)*

1 tsp mustard seeds

½ tsp asafoetida powder (hing)

1 cup well-packed mint leaves

1 cup grated fresh coconut

1 tsp salt or to taste

*1 marble-sized ball of tamarind,
without seeds or strings*

1. Heat oil in a frying pan over moderate heat. Add green chillies, dal, mustard seeds and asafoetida powder, and fry till dal turns golden and spices are fragrant.

2. Add mint leaves, fry for about 2 minutes and remove from heat.

3. Mix in coconut, salt and tamarind and grind to a smooth consistency, gradually adding ½ cup water.

4. Serve with any idli, dosai, vadai, adai or pakoda of choice.

variation: Substitute coriander leaves for mint to make **kothamalli chutney (coriander chutney).**

vengaya chutney
onion chutney

makes: ¾ cup
preparation time: 20 minutes
cooking time: 10 minutes

3 tbsp oil

2 tbsp pigeon peas (tuvar/arhar)

*2 tbsp husked bengal gram
(chana dal)*

*1 tbsp husked black gram
(urad dal)*

1 tsp mustard seeds

½ tsp asafoetida powder (hing)

2 dried red chillies

3 green chillies

*3 medium-sized onions, finely
chopped*

2 tbsp chopped coriander leaves

*1 marble-sized ball of tamarind,
without seeds or strings*

1 tsp salt or to taste

1. Heat 1 tbsp oil in a frying pan over low heat. Add all dals mustard seeds, asafoetida powder, red chillies and green chillies and fry till dal turns golden and spices and chillies are fragrant. Remove from heat and set aside.

2. Heat remaining oil in the same pan over moderate heat. Add onions and fry till golden. Combine all fried items with coriander leaves, tamarind and salt and grind to a smooth consistency. No water need be added.

3. Serve with any dosai, vadai, idli or adai of choice.

allam pachadi
ginger chutney from andhra pradesh

makes: ½ cup
preparation time: 5 minutes
cooking time: 3 minutes

1 tsp oil
3" piece ginger, grated
¼ tsp cumin seeds
4 dried red chillies
1 lime-sized ball of tamarind,
without seeds or strings
2 cloves garlic (optional)
2 tbsp powdered jaggery
½ tsp salt or to taste

tempering
1 tsp oil
½ tsp mustard seeds
½ tsp husked black gram
(urad dal)
1 dried red chilli, halved
1 sprig curry leaves

1. Heat oil in a frying pan over low heat. Add ginger, cumin seeds and red chillies and fry till fragrant.

2. Mix in tamarind, garlic (if used), jaggery and salt. Grind to a smooth consistency, gradually adding 2-3 tbsp water.

3. Heat oil for tempering in the same pan over moderate heat. Add remaining ingredients for tempering in the order given. When mustard seeds splutter, stir contents of pan into pachadi.

4. Serve with pesharattu (page 116).

cobri pachadi
coconut chutney from andhra pradesh

serves: 4-6
preparation time: 15 minutes
cooking time: 5 minutes

2 tsp oil

1 tsp husked black gram (urad dal)

1 tsp husked bengal gram
(chana dal)

2 dried red chillies

¼ tsp cumin seeds

4 cloves garlic (optional)

1 marble-sized ball of tamarind,
without seeds or strings

¼ tsp turmeric powder

1 cup cubed (¼" cubes) fresh
coconut

¾ tsp salt or to taste

1. Heat oil in a frying pan over moderate heat. Add dals, red chillies and cumin seeds. Fry till dals turn golden and chillies and cumin are fragrant.

2. Cool and mix in garlic, tamarind and turmeric powder. Grind to a coarse paste, gradually adding ¼ cup water.

3. Add coconut and ¼-½ cup water and grind again to a coarse paste. Sprinkle in salt and mix well.

4. Serve with atukula dosai (page 109) or any other dosai, or idli of choice.

Right : Clockwise from left bottom:
Alu gaddé bhath (page 92), kosu-carrot rasam (page 54), molakeerai poritha kuzhambu (page 31)
guthi bendakai (page 72), urulaikizhangu poriyal (papge 64), curd, payatha laddu (page 145),
fried appalam, clarified butter and karuvepillai thuvayal (page 158)

parupu thuvayal
green gram chutney from chettinad

serves: 4-6
preparation time: 10 minutes
cooking time: 5 minutes

½ cup husked green gram
(mung dal)
1 dried red chilli
1 clove garlic
1 tbsp grated fresh coconut
½ tsp salt or to taste

1. Roast dal in a dry frying pan over low heat, tossing frequently, for 5-7 minutes, till the raw aroma disappears.

2. Remove from heat and mix in remaining ingredients. Grind to a paste, gradually adding 2 tbsp water.

3. Serve with rice and ghee.

vazhathandu thuvayal
plantain stem chutney

serves: 4-6
preparation time: 20 minutes
cooking time: 10 minutes

2½ cups (1 foot long) chopped
plantain stem
¾ cup curd whisked with 2¼ cups
water
1 onion, finely chopped
2 green chillies
1 tbsp chopped mint leaves
2 tbsp chopped coriander leaves
1 marble-sized ball of tamarind,
without seeds or strings
1 tsp salt

tempering
1 tbsp oil
2 tsp mustard seeds
2 tbsp husked black gram (urad dal)
½ tsp asafoetida powder (hing)
3 dried red chillies

1. Soak plantain stem in diluted curd after chopping it, till required.

2. Heat oil for tempering in a frying pan over moderate heat. Add remaining ingredients for tempering in the order given. When mustard seeds splutter and dal turns pink, add onion. Sauté for about 2 minutes.

3. Drain plantain stem and add to pan with green chillies. Cover pan and simmer for 5-7 minutes till tender. Remove from heat and set aside till cool.

4. Mix in mint, coriander leaves, tamarind and salt. Grind to a fine paste without water.

5. Serve with rice.

Left : Parvaanam
(Rice dessert from Andhra Pradesh) see page 148

murungaikkai thuvayal
drumstick chutney

serves: 4-6
preparation time: 30 minutes
cooking time: 5 minutes

7-8 drumsticks, cut into 3" pieces
3 tsp oil
1 tsp mustard seeds
1 tsp husked black gram (urad dal)
1 tsp husked bengal gram
(chana dal)
2 dried red chillies
1 green chilli
½ tsp asafoetida powder (hing)
½ cup grated fresh coconut
2 tbsp chopped coriander leaves
¾ tsp salt or to taste
1 marble-sized ball of tamarind,
without seeds or strings

1. Place drumstick in a pan with 1½ cups water over high heat and bring to boil. Lower heat and simmer for 8-10 minutes till tender. Drain. Scrape out flesh and set aside.

2. Heat oil in a frying pan over moderate heat. Add mustard seeds, dals, red chillies, green chilli and asafoetida powder. Fry, tossing gently till dals turn golden and mustard seeds splutter. Remove from heat.

3. Mix in drumstick flesh, coconut, coriander leaves, salt and tamarind and grind to a fine paste without water.

4. Serve hot with rice and ghee. It can also be served with any dosai or idli of choice.

karuvepillai thuvayal
curry leaf chutney

makes: ½ cup
preparation time: 5 minutes
cooking time: 5 minutes

2 tsp oil
1 tsp mustard seeds
1 tbsp husked black gram
(urad dal)
2 dried red chillies
½ tsp asafoetida powder (hing)
1 cup well-packed curry leaves
½" piece ginger, grated
1 marble-sized ball of tamarind,
without seeds or string
1 tsp salt or to taste
2 tsp powdered jaggery

1. Heat oil in a frying pan over moderate heat. Add mustard seeds, dal, red chillies and asafoetida powder. Fry, tossing gently, till dal turns golden and spices are fragrant.

2. Remove from heat and mix in curry leaves, ginger, tamarind, salt and jaggery. Grind to a fine paste, gradually adding 2-3 tbsp water.

3. Serve with rice, or any dosai or idli of choice.

aratikai pachadi
green plantain chutney from andhra pradesh

serves: 4
preparation time: 10 minutes
cooking time: 10 minutes

1 large raw green plantain

¼ cup curd whisked with ¾ cup water

2 tsp oil

2 green chillies, finely chopped

1 marble-sized ball of tamarind, without seeds or strings

¾ tsp salt or to taste

tempering

3 tsp oil

½ tsp mustard seeds

½ tsp husked black gram (urad dal)

1 dried red chilli, halved

2 tbsp chopped onions

1 sprig curry leaves

1 tbsp chopped coriander leaves

1. Peel plantain, chop fine and soak in diluted curd till required.

2. Heat oil in a frying pan over moderate heat. Drain plantain and add to pan with green chillies. Fry for 8-10 minutes till plantain is tender.

3. Remove from heat, mix in tamarind and salt and grind to a coarse paste. Set aside.

4. Heat oil for tempering in a small pan over moderate heat. Add mustard seeds, dal and red chilli. When mustard seeds splutter, add onion and fry till golden. Stir in curry leaves and coriander leaves. Pour contents of pan into pachadi and mix well.

5. Serve with plain hot rice.

tengai thuvayal podi
spicy coconut powder

makes: 1 cup
preparation time: 15 minutes
cooking time: 5 minutes

2 tbsp oil
½ cup husked black gram
(urad dal)
½ cup husked bengal gram
(chana dal)
1 tbsp cumin seeds
8-10 dry red chillies
½ tsp asafoetida powder (hing)
2 cups grated fresh coconut
1 marble-sized ball of tamarind,
without seeds and strings
1 tsp salt or to taste

1. Heat 1 tbsp oil in a pan over moderate heat. Add dals and fry till golden. Remove from pan.

2. Heat remaining oil in the same pan and fry cumin seeds, red chillies and asafoetida for 1-2 minutes. Remove from heat.

3. Roast coconut in a dry frying pan over low heat till pink in colour. Remove from heat.

4. Mix all ingredients together and grind to a coarse powder.

5. Store in an airtight container and refrigerate.

6. Serve with rice and ghee.

dosai milagai podi
dosai chilli powder

makes: 2 cups
preparation time: 10 minutes
cooking time: 10 minutes

¼ cup husked black gram
(urad dal)
¼ cup husked bengal gram
(chana dal)
¼ cup white sesame seeds (til)
1 tsp asafoetida powder (hing)
½ cup grated dry coconut (copra)
2 tsp oil
1 cup dried red chillies
¼ cup roasted peanuts
1½ tsp salt or to taste
2 tbsp powdered jaggery

1. Roast dals, sesame seeds, asafoetida powder and copra separately in a dry frying pan, tossing gently. (Roast dals till they turn golden, and spices and copra till fragrant.)

2. Heat oil in the same pan and fry red chillies, tossing gently, till fragrant.

3. Combine all fried ingredients with remaining ingredients. Grind to a coarse powder.

4. This is an excellent accompaniment to dosai and idli.

malli thokku
coriander leaf powder from chettinad

makes: 1½ cups
preparation time: 10 minutes
cooking time: 10 minutes

1 tbsp oil
1 cup dried red chillies
½ cup husked black gram (urad dal)
1 large lemon-sized ball of tamarind, without seeds or strings
½ tsp asafoetida powder (hing)
2 cups chopped coriander leaves
1½ tsp salt or to taste

1. Heat a little oil at a time in a frying pan over low heat. Fry each ingredient separately, tossing gently. (Fry chillies till they change colour and dal till it turns pink. Toss tamarind for about a minute and asafoetida till fragrant. Mix coriander leaves with salt and toss for a minute.)

2. Combine all ingredients and grind to a coarse powder.

3. Store in an airtight container.

4. Serve with any dosai or idli of choice.

milagai karimeedu
green chilli and tamarind sauce

makes: about 1 cup
soaking time: 10 minutes
preparation time: 10 minutes
cooking time: 40-45 minutes

1 large lime-sized ball of tamarind
1 cup chopped green chillies
1½ tsp salt or to taste
3 tbsp powdered jaggery

tempering
2 tsp sesame oil (til ka tael)
1 tsp mustard seeds
½ tsp asafoetida powder (hing)
1 dried red chilli, halved
1 sprig curry leaves

1. Soak tamarind in 1½ cups water for 10 minutes. Extract juice and discard pulp.

2. Heat oil for tempering in a frying pan over moderate heat. Add remaining ingredients for tempering in the order given. When mustard seeds splutter, add green chillies and sauté for about 2 minutes.

3. Add tamarind juice, salt and jaggery. Simmer for 40-45 minutes till sauce thickens.

4. Serve with any dosai, idli or pongal of choice.

note: Leftover milagai karimeedu can be stored in a refrigerator for a week.

This delicious accompaniment is for those who like spice. It is a very hot sauce so use it judiciously.

vengaya gojju
shallot and tamarind curry

serves: 4-6
soaking time: 10 minutes
preparation time: 20 minutes
cooking time: 25 minutes

1 medium lime-sized ball of tamarind

½ cup shallots, peeled and kept whole

½ tsp turmeric powder

1 tsp salt or to taste

2 tbsp powdered jaggery

spice powder

2 tsp oil

5-6 dried red chillies

½ tsp asafoetida powder (hing)

2 tsp coriander seeds

¾ tsp fenugreek seeds (methi)

1 tsp husked bengal gram (chana dal)

tempering

2 tbsp sesame oil (til ka tael)

1 tsp mustard seeds

1 tsp husked black gram (urad dal)

1 dried red chilli, halved

1 sprig curry leaves

1. Soak tamarind in 2 cups water for 10 minutes. Extract juice and discard pulp.

2. Heat oil for spice powder in a pan. Add remaining ingredients for spice powder. Fry over low heat, tossing gently, till chillies and spices are fragrant and dal is golden. Cool and grind to a fine powder.

3. In the same pan heat oil for tempering over moderate heat. Add remaining ingredients for tempering in the order given. When mustard seeds splutter, add shallots and fry till golden.

4. Mix in tamarind juice, turmeric powder, salt and jaggery. Cover pan and simmer for 10-12 minutes, till the raw aroma of tamarind disappears.

5. Sprinkle in spice powder and simmer for another 10-12 minutes, stirring occasionally, till well blended and a little thick.

6. Serve hot with any dosai, idli or pongal of choice, as an accompaniment

note: You could use 2 finely chopped medium-sized onions if shallots are not available.

thakkali thokku
sweet and sour tomato jam

makes: about. ¾ cup
preparation time: 10 minutes
cooking time: 45 minutes

7-8 (500 gms) medium-sized
tomatoes, roughly chopped and
puréed
2 tbsp powdered jaggery
¾ tsp red chilli powder
1 tsp salt or to taste

tempering
2 tbsp sesame oil (til ka tael)
1 tsp mustard seeds
½ tsp asafoetida powder (hing)

1. Heat oil for tempering in a heavy-based frying pan over moderate heat. Add mustard seeds and asafoetida powder. When mustard seeds splutter, add tomato purée, jaggery, chilli powder and salt.

2. Simmer over low heat till tomato purée thickens to a jam-like consistency. Keep stirring to prevent it sticking to base of pan. All the moisture should evaporate and the thokku should be a dark maroon. This will take about 40-45 minutes.

3. Cool and store in a bottle in the refrigerator for up to a week.

4. Serve with any dosai, idli or adai of choice.

vegetable stew from kerala

serves: 3-4
preparation time: 20 minutes
cooking time: 20 minutes

2 cups grated coconut
1 tbsp coconut oil
1 bay leaf
2-3 cloves
2-3 green cardamoms
1" stick cinnamon
¼ cup shallots, peeled and kept
whole
1½ cups chopped (¼" pieces)
mixed vegetables – carrot, french
beans, potatoes – and green peas
and cauliflower florets
1 tsp salt or to taste

1. Mix grated coconut with 1 cup hot water. Process for 1-2 minutes in a blender. Pour liquid through a strainer lined with muslin cloth and press out thick coconut milk.

2. Add 1½ cups hot water to coconut residue. Blend and strain once more to get thin coconut milk.

3. Heat oil in a pan over moderate heat. Add bay leaf, cloves, cardamoms and cinnamon. Toss for a minute.

4. Add shallots and fry for about 2 minutes.

5. Mix in vegetables and stir-fry for another 2 minutes.

6. Add thin coconut milk and salt. Simmer for 10-12 minutes over low heat, till vegetables are tender.

7. Pour in thick coconut milk. Heat through on low heat, stirring continuously.

8. Serve hot with pathiri (page 131).

tengai thuvayal
brown coconut chutney

makes: ½-¾ cup
preparation time: 10 minutes
cooking time: 5 minutes

1 tbsp oil

2 tsp mustard seeds

2 dried red chillies

3 green chillies, chopped

½ tsp asafoetida powder (hing)

3-4 tsp husked bengal gram (chana dal)

1 tbsp husked black gram (urad dal)

½ cup grated fresh coconut

1 small marble-sized ball of tamarind, without seeds or strings

2 tbsp finely chopped coriander leaves

½ tsp salt or to taste

1. Heat oil in a frying pan over low heat. Add mustard seeds, red chillies, green chillies, asafoetida and dals and fry till dals turn golden.

2. Mix in remaining ingredients and grind to a fine paste, gradually adding 1½-2 tbsp water.

3. Serve with uppuma kozhakattay (page 140).

menthukura pachadi
fenugreek leaf chutney from andhra pradesh

makes: ½ cup
preparation time: 10 minutes
cooking time: 5 minutes

1½ tbsp oil

½ tsp husked bengal gram (chana dal)

½ tsp husked black gram (urad dal)

3 dried red chillies

½ tsp cumin seeds

½" piece ginger, grated

4 cloves garlic (optional)

1 sprig curry leaves

2 cups well-packed fresh fenugreek leaves, finely chopped

1 large tomato, finely chopped

1 tbsp finely chopped coriander leaves

¾ tsp salt or to taste

tempering

1 tsp oil

½ tsp mustard seeds

¼ tsp asafoetida powder (hing)

1 dried red chilli, halved

1. Heat ½ tbsp oil in a frying pan over low heat. Add dals red chillies and cumin seeds. Fry, tossing gently, till dals turn pink and chillies are fragrant. Remove from pan and set aside.

2. Pour remaining oil into pan and heat through. Add ginger, garlic, curry leaves and fenugreek leaves and fry for about 2 minutes.

3. Blend in tomato and cook till thick. Remove from heat.

4. Add all fried ingredients to pan and mix in coriander leaves and salt. Grind to a coarse paste without water.

5. Heat oil for tempering in a small pan over moderate heat. Add remaining ingredients for tempering in the order given. When mustard seeds splutter, pour contents of pan into chutney and mix well.

6. Serve with hot rice or any dosai of choice.

note: The souring agent used here is tomato. If you do not like the flavour of tomatoes, you can use tamarind instead. It will taste equally delicious.

suggested menus

menu 1
rice
verkadalai pitlay (page 22)
carrot poriyal (page 62)
nellikkai rasam (page 58)
pachaimilagai-kothamalli thayir pachadi (page 85)
curd

menu 2
rice
vengaya sambar (page 19)
elumichampazha rasam (page 48)
nellikai thayir pachadi (page 86)
urulaikizhangu poriyal (page 67)
curd

menu 3
rice
vendakkai puli kuzhambu (page 24)
kosu-carrot rasam (page 54)
moru keerai (page 79)
beetroot parupu usili (page 68)
curd

menu 4
rice
pakoda morukuzhambu (page 25)
goddu rasam (page 51)
urulaikizhangu poriyal (page 67)
kosu-pattani poricha kootu (page 77)
curd

menu 5
rice
thengai paal kuzhambu (page 36)
kollukai sathamadu (page 47)
yengai kathrikai kariamudhu (page 60)
urulaikizhangu thayir pachadi (page 84)
curd

menu 6
rice
molapappu (page 37)
mullakada charu (page 46)
guthi bendakkai (page 72)
aratikai pachadi (page 159)
curd

buffet spreads

menu 1

rice

roti, puri or any plain paratha

chepankizhangu paruppu kuzhambu (page 17)

cobbari paala pappucharu (page 56)

urulaikizhangu kurma (page 82)

senai urundai (page 73)

vazhakkai masala poriyal (page 61)

murungakeerai poriyal (page 66)

tengai sadam (page 96)

paravaannam – sweet (page 148)

curd

fried appalam

pickles

menu 2

rice

roti, puri or any plain paratha

tengaipaal morukuzhambu (page 26)

bellay saaru (page 57)

pudalangai poriyal (page 66)

kosu-pattani poricha kootu (page 77)

nellikai thayir pachadi (page 86)

bangala dumpa kurma (page 81)

godumai pulliyogaray (page 101)

aval payasam (page 147)

curd

fried appalam

pickles

glossary

english	hindi	tamil
almond	badam	baadam
amaranth leaves	cholai bhaaji	molaikeerai
asafoetida	hing	perungayam
ash gourd	petha	poosanikai
aubergine/brinjal/eggplant	baingan	kathirikkai
banana	kela	vazhaikkai
basil – wild/ram/holy	tulsi	thulasi
bay leaf	tej patta	brinji elai
beetroot	chukandar	beetroot
bengal gram		
–flour	besan	kadalai mavu
–husked	chana dal	kadalai parupu
–roasted	bhuna chana	pottu kadalai
–whole	kala chana	konda kadalai
bitter gourd	karela	pagarkai
black gram		
–husked	urad dal	ulutham parupu
–whole	sabut urad	muzhu ulundu
black pepper	kali mirch	milagu
bread	double roti	roti
butter	makhan	vennai
–clarified	ghee	nei
cabbage	bund gobhi	muttaikos
capsicum/bell pepper	shimla mirch	kudamilagai
cardamom		
–green	hari elaichi/chhoti elaichi	elakkai
–black	badi elaichi	periya elakkai
carrot	gaajar	carrot
cashew nut	kaju	mundiri parupu
cauliflower	phool gobhi	kovippu, cauliflower
chickpeas	kabuli chana	kothukadalai
chilli		
–dry red	sookhi mirch	vatral milagai
–green	hari mirch	pachai milagai
choko	chow chow	bangalore kathirikai
cinnamon	dalchini	lavanga pattai
cloves	laung	krambu

english	hindi	tamil
cluster beans	gwar ki phalli	kothavarangai
coconut		
–dry (copra)	kopra	coparai
–fresh	nariyal	tengai
–milk	nariyal ka doodh	tengai pal
colocasia	arbi	chepankizhangu
coriander		
–leaves	hara dhania	kothamalli
–seeds	dhania	kothamalliverai/dhania
corn	makkai	cholam
cowpeas	lobia	karamani
cream	malai	aadai
cumin seeds	jeera	jeeragam
–black cumin	kala/shah jeera	karunjeeragam
curd/yoghurt	dahi	thayir
curry leaf	kari patta	karivepilai
drumsticks	surjan ki phalli	murungaikkai
–leaves	surjan ki saag	murungaikeerai
elephant yam	zimikand/sooran	chenai kizhangu
finger millet	mohua/madua	ragi
fennel seeds	badi saunf	sombu
fenugreek		
–leaves	methi bhaaji	vendayakeerai
–seeds	methi saag	vendayam
french beans	fransbin	beans
garlic	lassun	poondu
ginger		
–fresh	adrak	inji
–powder	saunth	sukku
green gram		
–husked	moong dal	payatham parupu
– whole	sabut mung	pachai payaru
green peas	mattar	pattani
horse gram	kulthi ka dal	kollukai
indian gooseberry	amla	nellikai
jackfruit (unripe)	kathal	palakkai
jaggery	gur	vellam
lime	nimbu	elumichampazham
mango		
–table	aam	mambazham

english	hindi	tamil
–unripe	aam	mangai
margosa flower	neem ka phool	vepampoo
milk	doodh	paal
mint	pudina	pudina
mustard seeds	sarson/rai	kadugu
nutmeg	jaiphal	jhadhikkai
okra/ladies' fingers	bhindi	vendaikkai
onion	pyaaz	vengayam
peanut/groundnut	mungphali	verkadalai
pigeon peas	arhar/tuvar	tuvaram parupu
pistachio	pista	pista
plantain	kela	vazhaikkai
–cooking	kela	vazhaikkai
–flower	mocha	vazha poo
–stem		vazha thandu
poppy seeds	khus-khus	khasa khasa
potato	alu	urulaikizhangu
pumpkin		
–red	seetaphul/kuddu	parangikai
radish		
–white	safaid mooli	mullangi
raisin – seedless	kishmish	dhratchai
rice	chaval	arisi
–broken	tukda chaval	arisi noi
–flour	chaval ka atta	arisi mavu
–parboiled	ukda/sela	puzhungal arisi
–parched	poha	aval
ridge gourd	toori	peerkangai
saffron	kesar	kungumappu
sago	sabudana	jawarisi
salt	namak	uppu
semolina	rava/sooji	ravai
sesame – oil	til ka tael	nalla ennai
–seeds	til	ellu
shallot	sambar/madras pyaaz	china vengayam/
		sambar vengayam
sheet beans	saem	avarakkai
snake gourd	chirchinda	pudalangai
sodium bicarbonate	meetha soda	samayal soda/soda uppu
spinach	palak	pasala keerai

english	hindi	tamil
sugar	cheeni	chakkarai
tamarind	imli	puli
tomato	tamatar	thakkali
turmeric	haldi	manjal
vermicelli	sevian	semiya
wheat	gehun	godumai
–broken	daliya	godumai rava/noi
–lapsi	daliya	odacha godumai
–plain/refined flour	maida	maida
–whole flour	atta	godumai mavu
–whole grains	gehun	godumai
yam	zimikand	senai

notes:

ajwain: It is an umbelliferous plant which grows in India and the Far East. It is sometimes referred to as carom seeds, and belongs to the same family as the Ethiopian bishop's weed and English lovage. It is called omum in Tamil.

amla: The botanical name for amla is *Emblica officinalis*. It is a jade-green, tart fruit also known as the emblic gooseberry or Indian hog plum. It is called nellikai in Tamil.

khoya: Unsweetened, dried, condensed, milk made by cooking milk, stirring constantly, till it forms a heavy, thick granular lump. It is also called khoya in Tamil.

marathi moggu: A spice resembling a large clove, it is used in Karnataka and Andhra.

tulsi: Sometimes called holy basil, Ram basil or wild basil, it belongs to the basil family and is regarded as a holy plant in India. It is called thulasi in Tamil.